BORO & SASHIKO
Harmonious Imperfection

The Art of Japanese Mending & Stitching

Shannon & Jason Mullett-Bowlsby, the Shibaguyz

stashBOOKS®

an imprint of C&T Publishing

Text and photography copyright © 2020 by Shannon & Jason Mullett-Bowlsby

Photography and artwork copyright © 2020 by C&T Publishing, Inc.

Publisher: Amy Barrett-Daffin

Creative Director: Gailen Runge

Acquisitions Editor: Roxane Cerda

Managing Editor: Liz Aneloski

Editor: Karla Menaugh

Technical Editor: Debbie Rodgers

Cover/Book Designer: April Mostek

Production Coordinator: Tim Manibusan

Production Editor: Jennifer Warren

Illustrator: Valyrie Gillum

Photo Assistants: Kaeley Hammond and Lauren Herberg

Instructional photography by Jason Mullett-Bowlsby; lifestyle and subjects photography by Estefany Gonzalez of C&T Publishing, Inc., unless otherwise noted

Library of Congress Cataloging-in-Publication Data

Names: Mullett-Bowlsby, Shannon, author. | Mullett-Bowlsby, Jason, author.

Title: Boro & sashiko, harmonious imperfection : the art of Japanese mending & stitching / Shannon & Jason Mullett-Bowlsby, the Shibaguyz.

Other titles: Boro and sashiko, harmonious imperfection

Description: Lafayette, CA : Stash Books, an imprint of C&T Publishing, Inc., 2020. | Includes bibliographical references and index.

Identifiers: LCCN 2020027229 | ISBN 9781617459191 (trade paperback) | ISBN 9781617459207 (ebook)

Subjects: LCSH: Sashiko--Patterns. | Patchwork--Patterns. | Stitches (Sewing)

Classification: LCC TT835 .M8238 2020 | DDC 746.46/041--dc23

LC record available at https://lccn.loc.gov/2020027229

Printed in China

0 9 8 7 6 5

Dedication

TO ANOREE KAY BRUNER-BOWLSBY, ALSO KNOWN AS MOM

As a lifelong maker, you always cheered us on and celebrated our accomplishments in the fiber arts. When we found out we were going to be writing a sewing book, you were the first one we wanted to call. We hope we did you proud.

—J & S

Acknowledgments

SEATTLE ART MUSEUM   We are eternally grateful to the folx at the Seattle Art Museum, particularly Elisabeth Smith (Collection and Provenance Associate) and Marta Pinto-Llorca (Senior Collections Care Manager). Thank you for having faith in our vision and for giving us supervised access to study the pristine pieces that allowed us to confirm our theories and learn amazing new things about boro and sashiko.

ROLAND CRAWFORD—ANCIENT GROUNDS   Special thanks to our new friend for sharing part of his epic boro collection. His generosity gave us a deeper understanding of the imperfect beauty and genius of centuries-old boro. A visit to his coffee shop in Seattle, Ancient Grounds, is a rabbit hole into history ... and he makes a mean latte (just sayin'!).

CHRISTINE C.   You were our eyes and ears in Japan. We can't thank you enough for sourcing thread, thimbles, needles, and thread snips for us to compare to our United States tools. And the books you brought back were true treasures.

Shannon examining a garment at the Seattle Art Museum

RESOURCES   Thank you to the following companies, which generously provided products for use in the creation of this book: Aurifil, BERNINA of America, Clover Needlecraft, Reliable Corporation, Cherrywood Fabrics, Marcus Fabrics, Michael Miller Fabrics, RJR Fabrics, and Robert Kaufman Fabrics.

THOSE WHO CAME BEFORE US   We thank those whose hands created the work that inspired us. Their work, created from necessity, now inspires scores of crafters to emulate and reawaken this art form. We hope our efforts to carry on and translate their work honor their existence and their lives.

CONTENTS

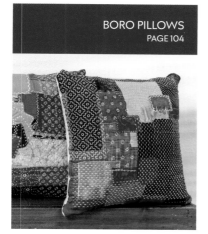

BORO PILLOWS
PAGE 104

REVERSIBLE KNOT BAG
PAGE 108

TOO CUTE FOR THE
GROCERIES TOTE
PAGE 114

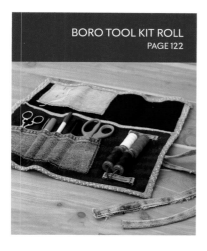

BORO TOOL KIT ROLL
PAGE 122

SASHIKO SAMPLER
WALLHANGING
PAGE 128

RECTANGLE WRAP VEST
PAGE 134

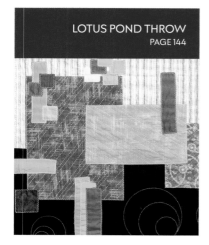

LOTUS POND THROW
PAGE 144

KIMONO-INSPIRED
LONG JACKET
PAGE 150

HANTEN SHORT JACKET
PAGE 158

Sashiko Stitch Visual Guide

Running Stitches

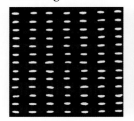

Stacked Running
Stitches   85

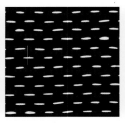

Offset Running
Stitch   85

Offset Crosses and Variations

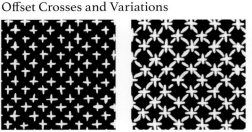

Offset Crosses
86

Rice Stitch
86

Rice Stitch
Variation 1   87

Offset Crosses and Variations *continued*

Rice Stitch Variation 2
(4–Way Cross)   87

Zigzag Crosses
88

Chained Crosses
88

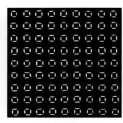

Boxes
89

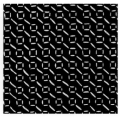

Boxes Variation 1
89

Persimmon Flower and Variations

Persimmon Flower
90

Double Persimmon
Flower   90

Mountain Form
91

Mountain Form
Variation   91

Hitomezashi Stitches Without Crossing Stitches

Rice Flower Stitch
92

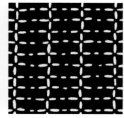

Stacked Lines
92

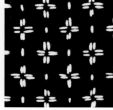

Stacked Lines
Variation   93

Star Stitch
93

Woven Patterns

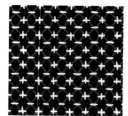

Woven Pattern 1   94

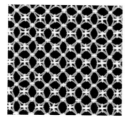

Woven Pattern 2   94

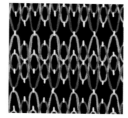

Woven Pattern 3   95

MOYOUZASHI STITCHES

Straight-Line Patterns

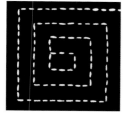

Spiral
96

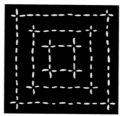

Concentric Squares
96

Circular Patterns

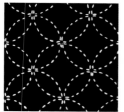

Linked Seven
Treasures   97

Blue Ocean Waves
97

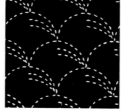

Blowing Grasses
98

Pinwheels
98

Diamond Patterns

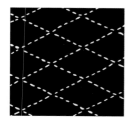

Diamonds
99

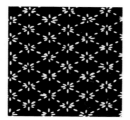

Diamonds Variation 1
99

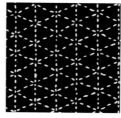

Woven Bamboo
100

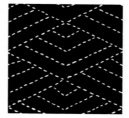

Diamond Blue Waves
100

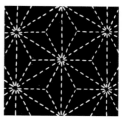

Asanoha (Hemp Leaf)
101

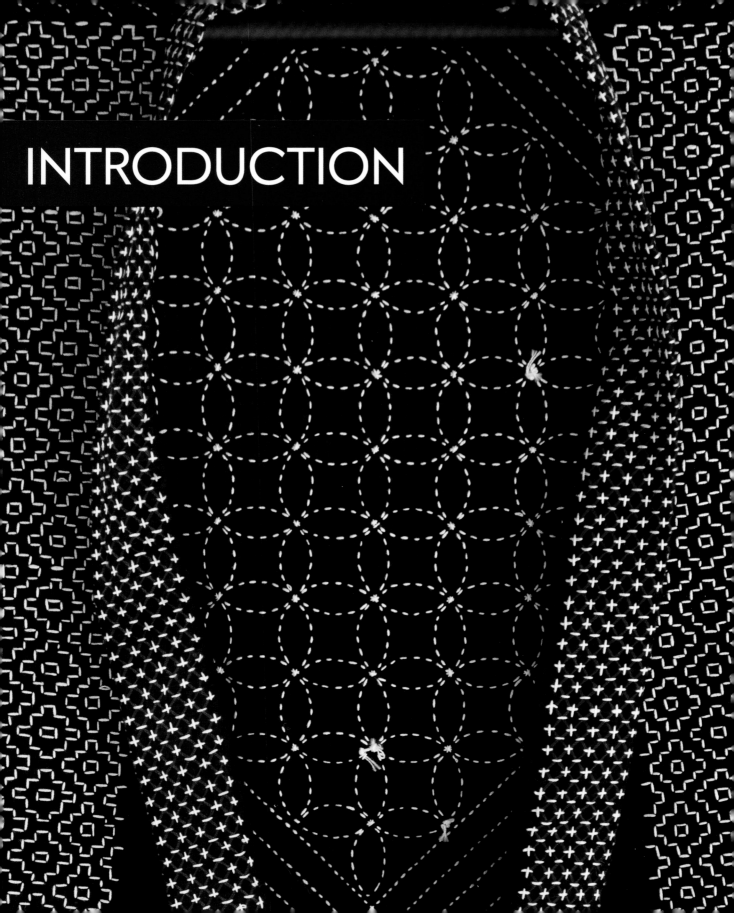

INTRODUCTION

Time Travel Through Fabric, Craft, and Art—Welcome to the Rabbit Hole

We are rabbit-hole people. We love research and finding out the story behind things. We get a thought in our heads or come across an idea, and the next thing you know there are 120 browser windows open on several devices and we've checked out every book and downloaded every documentary on the subject. No subject is too great or too small that we won't dive right down that rabbit hole until our curiosity is satisfied. Sometimes that takes minutes; sometimes it takes days or years.

Our journey in boro and sashiko started innocently enough while researching patch-work and handwork techniques that didn't require much equipment and, ideally, would be completely portable. In the hopes that we could develop future classes that would inspire others to do more handwork, we began to build on our own skills of hand sewing, hand-pieced quilting, and English paper piecing.

As one does when one is going down a rabbit hole, we took a random turn. This new path led us to the history of crazy quilts—something we were familiar with from family members who had made at least one of these glorious quilts.

But where that turn lead to was completely unexpected. And wonderful.

Always focused on the context of the content (the heart that beats within the chest of every rabbit-hole person), we researched the origins of crazy quilts, which lead us to stumble onto an article with a vague reference to the Philadelphia Centennial Exhibition of 1876 and a display from the newly "opened" Japan that included repaired pottery and textiles. Another browser window and search-engine inquiry resulted in historical documents that referenced these patched and repaired textiles and pottery as the impetus for the crazy quilts movement of the late nineteenth century. Patched Japanese textiles—that sounded interesting! We wanted to see where that went.

Several more browser tabs and there it was on our computer screen: the front page of the Amuse Museum in Japan with its permanent exhibit of boro pieces collected by Chuzaburo Tanaka. We had never seen boro or sashiko textiles before, but here they were in all their unassuming glory. Each piece was tattered and patched and adorned with elaborate stitching, all done by hand for the purpose of strengthening and repairing the fabrics. They were glorious!

Even more deep dives and hundreds of books and web pages later, we found ourselves utterly consumed with how the boro and sashiko techniques were closely tied to hand stitching and repairing techniques from all over the world, including those from our own backgrounds. This was all new and exciting but strangely familiar and comfortable. We found ourselves remembering patched blankets and clothes from our childhoods. And even as recently as 25 years ago, as a younger married couple, we remembered patching up work clothes to make them last longer because we couldn't afford to buy new ones.

As we studied the textiles in person in private collections and in the archives of the Seattle Art Museum, and our hands practiced the stitching techniques (this was literally

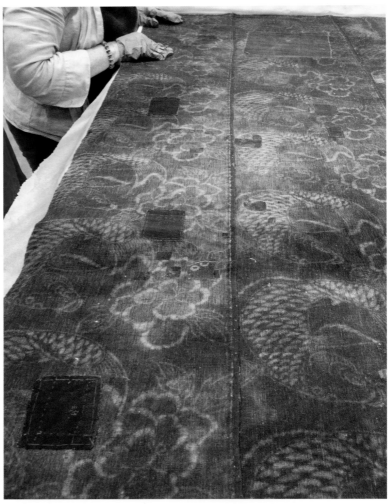

A large textile panel with boro patches being examined by staff at the Seattle Art Museum

not our grandmother's running stitch), we delved deeper into the world of the Japanese people who created these pieces. What were their lives like that they, over the course of lifetimes, were required to patch garments and blankets and hand them down, each generation making subsequent patches and repairs? Why were these textiles created in the first place? The answers spurred a deeper obsession for boro and sashiko—a love that has led us to learn more and seek out instructors and collectors from whom we can continue to learn.

These techniques—which started from a utilitarian practice, dire necessity, and destitution—have, through the passage of time, become art. Like looking at our grandma's and great-grandma's quilts and handwork pieces, looking at these boro pieces transports us back to a time and place that seems surreal in the context of our relatively comfortable lives. We have a difficult time fathoming the daily life of these people who first laid hands on this fabric. Who were they? What were they thinking about when making these stitches? Did they quietly sing songs to themselves like we do when we work in our studios? This connection with the original makers and their lives, their worlds, this is the transportive nature of studying these textiles from another place and time.

Time travel through fabric, craft, and art. Indeed, it is through the passage of time that this necessary and utilitarian practice has become art.

Our hope is that you will experience at least a portion of the joy we have found in the connection to a new way of looking at our handwork, and, through the projects we have created, find your own joy and freedom to create something new and exciting.

- -

THE STITCHER'S PROMISE

Raise your needle and repeat:

I, *[insert your name here]*, do promise to be patient with myself and not judge my work harshly. I promise to remind myself of the *fact* that every new skill has a learning curve everyone must go through, regardless of how accomplished they are at other skills.

- -

A panel of boro fabric from the collection of Roland Crawford

A utilitarian practice, after the passage of time, can be observed as art.

A WORD (OR TWO) ABOUT BORO AND SASHIKO

A Little Context for the Content

Examining the collection of Roland Crawford at Ancient Grounds

BORO: From Japanese *boroboro*, meaning "rags"

"Boro is patched clothing with a lot of small cloths here and there, but nothing fancy like today's quilted or patched works. It was made purely for the practical purposes for retaining warmth in the snowy areas and for making it last as long as possible where it was hard to obtain any sorts of cloth. When we review its practicality and design from today's point of view, we are able to realize its incredible sophistication." —Amuse Museum

To hear the word *boro* spoken can bring up many connotations. Our Japanese students and friends would indicate that they aren't dressing up by saying they were just wearing *boroboro*, meaning their old clothes, nothing fancy. A quick internet search (there's that rabbit hole again) will bring up information about patched textiles primarily from nineteenth and early twentieth century Japan. But that same search also will bring up boro as a sewing technique to patch textiles and to make layered patchwork-style textiles for quilts, garments, home appliqué, and accessories. Whether you think of boro as a noun (patched textiles), a verb (the act of sewing patches to worn fabric), or an adjective (old worn-out fabrics) is all in the way you look at it. For this book we will refer to boro as both the act (or art) of patching textiles and creating new textiles with layered patchwork.

First, a little history lesson:

Boro was practiced for the most part in northernmost areas of Japan where the harsh climate, shortage of supplies, and deep poverty (compared to the cities where the ruling class lived) made it a necessity for villagers to save the supplies they had at hand to repair and insulate their clothing. The cold climate and short growing season of the region made it impossible to grow their own cotton for weaving and spinning, and the socio-political climate was just as cold to these farmers and fishers. Considered lower-class citizens, the inhabitants of this northern region were legally prohibited from wearing brightly colored cloth, silk, and, more specifically, cotton from the south. The penalty for violating this law was severe and included public execution.

A boro jacket/hanten from the collection of Roland Crawford

Cloth and thread for clothes, blankets, and household goods were fabricated from indigenous plants like flax, ramie, or hemp. The fabric woven from these rough fibers was not very sturdy and did very little to ward off the effects of the elements.

To help strengthen these fabrics, folx dyed them with a plant-based dye called indigo. Once indigo was set and oxidized, it resulted in a rich, blue-colored fabric—a color approved by the Shogunate (the ruling class) for wear by the working class. Despite the obvious beauty of indigo, its appeal is not just aesthetics. Indigo brings qualities to cloth that made it sought after not just by the working class but by the Samurai as well. Indigo saturates the fibers and makes them stronger, odor resistant, dirt resistant, antibacterial, and insect repellent. Firefighters wore garments dyed with indigo because of its flame-retardant qualities. Indigo is nearly magical in the qualities it instills on fabric!

However, wear and tear do take a toll. This is where boro patches and sashiko stitching came into play. The average farmer or fisher would own very few garments over the course of a lifetime. There simply were no options for purchasing new clothing, and resources for making new garments were scarce. The most reasonable option was to repair the threadbare or torn garment. Scraps of fabric, some we studied as small as a dime, were layered and sewn into place with straight lines of stitches or sashiko motifs to create thicker, warmer garments and blankets. The original boro textiles involved no real planning beyond the fact that, when a hole or a weakness in the fabric was discovered, a patch was added with stitching for reinforcement. Even so, the resulting textiles are stunning.

Antique boro piece from the collection of Roland Crawford, Ancient Grounds, and a detail of the Too Cute for the Groceries Tote (page 114)

During our supervised research at the Seattle Art Museum, we had the privilege of viewing a number of garments that were more than a century old. Some of these pieces, obviously ceremonial garments, were in pristine condition. Others, made from more rustic fibers, displayed the telltale signs of wear and the resulting boro patches on the inside of the garment. Every time we found another patch, we, and the curators of the museum, would give out a little gasp (okay, sometimes it was a full-on scream). Our hands-on inspection of pieces from the private collection of Roland Crawford gave us insight into garments patched and stitched by actual working folx. These garments were layered with patches to the point that we had to work through them to find the original base fabrics. Regardless of origin—ceremonial fineries or rural work wear—the textiles that emerge as a result of the layering patchwork of boro have a kind of unselfconscious beauty and artisanship that is enthralling.

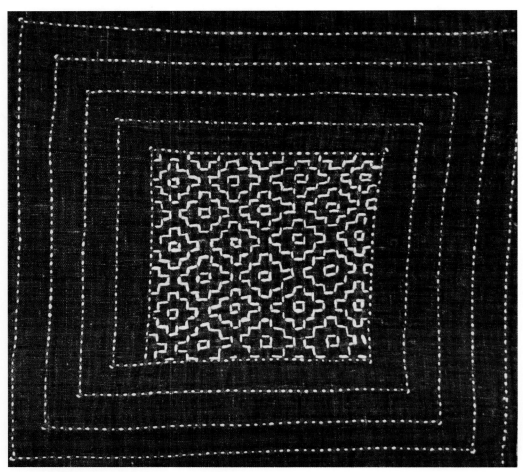

From the Seattle Art Museum Asian art collection

Sashiko: The "Little Stabs"

If we are going to talk about boro, we have to include sashiko in the conversation. Because, while sashiko can exist without boro, boro cannot exist without sashiko—the stitches that hold the boro patches in place.

Literally translated, *sashiko* means "little stabs," and that is exactly what it is. Sashiko refers to the small running stitches that were used to attach the boro patches to the garment and to strengthen weak fabrics or areas of intense wear. These stitches could be sewn in straight lines, symbols, motifs, pictures, or without thought as to how they appeared. The ultimate goal of sashiko was to secure, strengthen, and embellish.

Constructed of rough plant fibers and woven on rustic looms, the cloth of the working classes was loosely woven. The addition of white ramie thread would in no small manner reweave the fabric, which helped close up the holes in the base cloth, and also secure additional layers of fabric, which added warmth in a harsh climate. For these farmers and fishers, the main purpose of boro and sashiko was to make cloth thicker, warmer, and more durable.

Now we can look back at sashiko through the lens of time and with socio-political distance, and we can see the beauty and even the art of this utilitarian practice. The main religion of Japan was Shinto Buddhism, in which every natural element, object, person, plant, and animal is imbued with *kami*, or spirit. Representing a natural element, plant, or object in stitching transferred the powers and properties of those elements and objects to the wearer, as in the examples that follow.

Asanoha, the hemp leaf sashiko pattern, represents good fortune, good health, and growth.

Yamagata, a mountain form sashiko pattern, gifts the wearer with strength and steadfastness.

Seigaiha, a waves sashiko pattern, produces the effect of resilience, tranquility, and the ability to literally "go with the flow."

Although there are regional variations to each, sashiko can be grouped into three main forms:

HITOMEZASHI SASHIKO   Hitomezashi-style sashiko is based on a grid with patterns developing from intersecting and crossing lines of stitches.

MOYOUZASHI SASHIKO   Moyouzashi-style sashiko patterns are based on simple straight or curved lines using as many stitches as needed to get from one point to another. Stitches may be counted, but lines of moyouzashi stitches never cross on the front of the fabric.

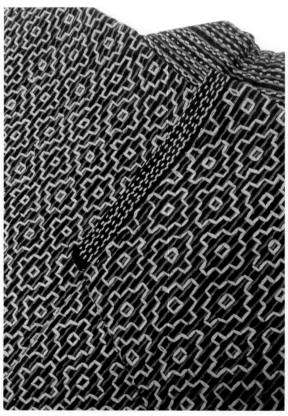

An example of hitomezashi sashiko worked over a kimono, from the Seattle Art Museum's Asian art collection

An example of moyouzashi sashiko, showing the curved lines following pre-drawn shapes, from the Seattle Art Museum's Asian art collection

KOGIN-ZASHI   *Kogin* means "small cloth" and *zashi* means "stitches." Kogin is a form of counted embroidery, in which elaborate designs of geometric patterns are created by counting the number of threads in the base fabric that are sewn over or under. It is worked one row at a time using the warp and weft threads to create a grid upon which the Kogin motifs are built.

Kogin patterns are made up of smaller elements called *modoko*. These modoko are combined to make larger, complex motifs and overall fabric patterns that are the defining characteristic of Kogin-zashi. Kogin is a study in and of itself with an entire agency—the Hirosaki Kogin Research Institute—dedicated solely to the research and preservation of this particular sashiko technique.

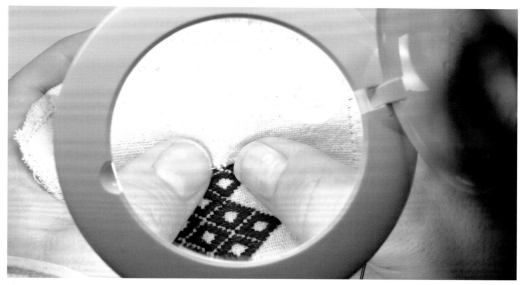

Shannon practicing Kogin–zashi sashiko, used to fill the spaces of loosely woven fabric

Regardless of style, sashiko stitch patterns are made using the running stitch. Further, they are created by loading the fabric onto the needle and creating many stitches (sometimes an entire row) at one time. The fabric is loaded onto the needle, then pushed through the fabric using a palm thimble. The fabric then is pulled all at once along the length of the thread and smoothed out, ensuring that the thread is neither puckering the fabric nor that is it too loose.

All sashiko stitches are made without a hoop, with the fabric and thread tension maintained entirely by hand. This does take a bit of practice but, once you have achieved the dexterity and rhythm, it is relaxing and even meditative.

Throughout this book we will be using a combination of hitomezashi and moyouzashi stitches to secure our boro patches, strengthen the fabrics, and embellish the projects.

Into the Modern Day

The practice of boro continued in rural areas of northern Japan through the Meiji Era well into Imperial Japan. As laws about trade loosened and roads and railway connected these areas to urban centers, allowing for increased trade and wealth to pour in, the act of boro became a much maligned and shameful act. The suggestion that any working-class citizen was ever so impoverished was actively hidden by the government and by individual families. As a result, generations worth of boro items were stuffed into walls as insulation, concealed under floorboards, and put away in barns and outbuildings. The stories and artwork of these unique textiles disappeared as they themselves slowly decayed. The art form would no doubt have died without so much as a whimper had it not been for the work of one man: Chuzaburo Tanaka.

Tanaka was one of the first people to recognize boro as an art form of cultural significance. He traveled throughout rural Japan searching through attics and barns, under floorboards, and inside the walls of buildings to find hidden boro treasures. His work yielded a collection of more than 20,000 pieces of boro, including 786 items now designated as Important Tangible Cultural Properties by the Japanese government. Boro items salvaged by Tanaka are on permanent display at the Textile Culture and Ukiyo-e Art Museum, also known as the Amuse Museum, in Tokyo. Included in this exhibit are works by modern designers like Louis Vuitton as examples of how boro textiles have been incorporated into their modern garment design. The contribution of Chuzaburo Tanaka to the modern researcher of boro textiles cannot be overstated—including the work of these two grateful researchers.

HERE WE ARE TODAY

When we began to research this book, one of goals was to bring this art form into the twenty-first century while being respectful of its history. We wanted to present our content with context. No short order.

On the off chance that we could get in, we sent a hopeful email to the textiles department of the Seattle Art Museum (SAM). SAM has an extensive collection of Asian art; in fact, they have an entire stand-alone Asian Art Museum. We were invited to view fifteen pristine garments from their Asian art collection, including some that had never been displayed. After hoping to view one or two pieces, this was our wildest dream come true! We'd be the first people to see these pieces in almost a century! Much rejoicing was had in the Mullett-Bowlsby household that day....

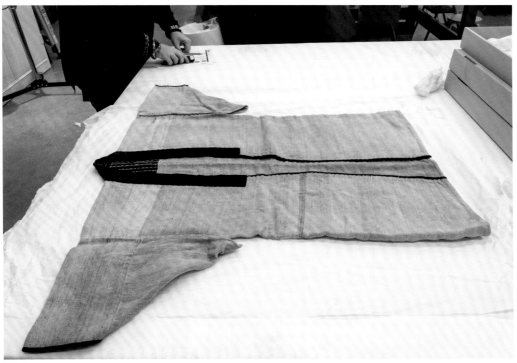

Workman's hanten, viewed in the archives of the Seattle Art Museum

While we were viewing those garments, Marta, the senior collections care manager, mentioned that she had a friend who had collected old, tattered garments and fabric pieces over a lifetime of trips to Japan. He had a literal stack of boro items in his coffee shop ... right across the street from the museum. ... I'm pretty sure that Shannon actually squealed in delight (confirmed as fact: he did). Marta set up a meeting with Roland and a few months later we had exhaustively looked over both collections multiple times and were able to review and compare actual boro and sashiko fabrics from the eighteenth, nineteenth, and twentieth centuries and some that could not be exactly dated because of their state of wear. We gained first-hand knowledge of fabrics, construction techniques, sizing, direction of work—even whether or not to tie knots in the end of sashiko lines. (We'd been taught to never tie knots. Our documentation: There were knots *all over* the inside!)

We can't emphasize enough the importance to us that, while we work these projects with our hands and minds, we create with context—keeping our hearts connected with reverence and respect to the art of boro and sashiko and the people who used it for their very survival.

On the following pages is the result of our desire to study and replicate the essence of boro patchwork. The original was done out of necessity but, through the lens of time, we are able to see the seemingly random patches and the resulting textiles as works of art.

THE TOOLS

One of the most appealing aspects of sashiko and boro is the minimal need for tools. Here we include the essentials as well as some of our most-used tools to enhance your boro and sashiko kits.

The Main Tools

▌NEEDLES

The first thing you will notice when you pick up a sashiko needle is how large they are. Especially if you are used to handling sharps or betweens, these needles are going to feel like a harpoon in comparison. Sashiko needles are anywhere from 2¼″ to 2½″ (5.7 to 6.4 cm) long and have a thick shaft, large eye, and a long, sharp point. The long shaft is ideal for loading the fabric onto, the thickness of the sashiko thread makes it necessary for the eye of the needle to be larger, and the long, sharp point makes it easier to push through thick or dense fabrics. In addition, the long taper of the sharp point makes it more likely that you will go through the weave of the fabric than through the threads, causing them to break and fray.

Shorter and longer sashiko needles from Japan

Three lengths of sashiko needles from Clover

THE FESTIVAL OF BROKEN NEEDLES

In Shinto Buddhism, Hari-Kuyō, the Festival of Broken Needles, was first practiced around 400 years ago. It is held once a year as a way for sewists— both professionals and hobbyists—to pay homage to and thank their tools for their service and to ask for improved skills in the year ahead.

▌THIMBLE WITH PALM PLATE

Sashiko thimbles are specialized for the hand actions needed to complete sashiko stitches. The thimble is actually an adjustable ring that you place around your middle finger with the disc laying on the pad of your hand. The disc protects your palm as you push the threaded needle through the fabric. The dimples in the disc help hold the eye of the needle in place as your thumb and middle finger hold it securely.

Thimble with palm plate from Japan

Clover thimble with palm plate

The disc lies against the pad of your hand, just below your finger.

▌THREAD

Sashiko thread is a plied, non-separating cotton thread. Unlike 6-ply embroidery thread that you separate depending on the thickness you need, sashiko thread is used in multiple strands to achieve the desired thickness. The thread we used throughout this book is from our own 12-weight FAB Sashiko Essentials thread collection by Aurifil. We hold it double for all of the stitching in our projects unless otherwise indicated.

Traditional sashiko threads from Japan

The Shibaguyz' FAB Sashiko Essentials thread collection by Aurifil

Other Tools

FABRIC SCISSORS AND APPLIQUÉ SCISSORS   A nice, heavy pair of fabric scissors is a must-have for working with large cuts of fabric and taking apart garments to be repurposed as patches and textile components. Bonus: Your appliqué scissors can double as thread scissors. *fig. A*

THREAD SNIPS   Traditional Japanese thread snips are exactly what you need for a quick snip. We use hand-forged snips from Japan and our Clover Kuroha thread snips. These have lasted for years and can even be sharpened. *fig. B*

ROTARY CUTTERS   Large rotary cutters often are easier to use than scissors for making smooth, quick cuts—especially on curves. *fig. C*

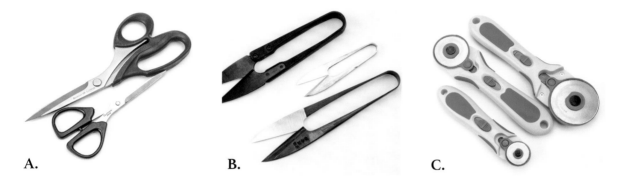

A.　　　　　**B.**　　　　　**C.**

PINS AND CLIPS   Quilting pins, appliqué pins, patchwork pins, and Wonder Clips ... they all work, and you will use them for these projects, but we highly recommend picking up a couple of boxes of coiless safety pins. Large pieces of fabric can shift while stitching without a frame, as we do in boro and sashiko. Basting layers together with coiless safety pins holds them in place securely without snagging the fabric. *fig. D*

ART AND DRAFTING TEMPLATES   We use these templates for circles, squares, triangles, and hexagons for the majority of our sashiko pattern drawing. *fig. E*

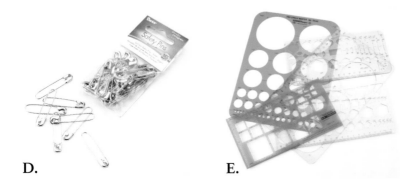

D.　　　　　**E.**

QUILTING TEMPLATES AND RULERS   Quilting templates are handy guides for marking single or repeating shapes. We used a set of circular templates to create the abstract lotus-flower shapes in the Lotus Pond Throw *(page 144)*. We use quilting rulers to measure the seams on patterns, and they make short work of the seemingly Herculean task of marking the stitching lines for an entire garment panel or throw. *fig. F*

PLASTIC CANVAS GRID   These sheets of perfectly arranged holes make easy-to-follow grids; just use your marking pens to fill in those holes. We mostly use the block grids but also have used the round grid to mark concentric circles. *fig. G*

CANS, GLASSES, AND BOXES   If it has a smooth edge and you can run a pencil, pen, or marker around it, you can use it for marking. Cookie cutters? Coffee cans? Coffee mugs and wine glasses? Yup! *fig. H*

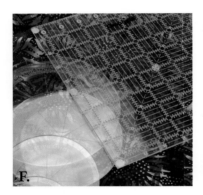
F.

G.

H.

DISAPPEARING-INK PENS   We have tested a lot of disappearing ink products. Our most consistent results have come from the White Marking Pens (Fine) by Clover. They make a crisp, clear line on dark fabrics, and a quick pass with an iron is all it takes for the marks to vanish before your eyes. For light fabrics, we prefer Clover's Water-Erasable Marker in blue. It makes a clear line and comes out with a light wash. *fig. I*

I.

Tip: Test Your Pens, Pencils, and Markers

With any marking utensil, *test your fabric before you mark it up* to ensure the ink performs its disappearing act. We mark our test fabric with several lines, then leave it to set in overnight. If we can still press, wash, or erase the lines out the next day, we're all set!

Sample being pressed to make lines disappear

PENCILS   We were delighted to discover that a standard drawing pencil from our art kit worked beautifully on a light-colored fabric. The two we keep on hand are a Palomino HB with a white eraser and a General's 6B. *fig. J*

OTHER MARKING TOOLS   We use white charcoal pencils on darker fabrics when we want to sketch out a design or test the layout of our patches. For example, we drew in the patches on the Hanten Short Jacket *(page 158)* to see placement ahead of time, helping us make design decisions quickly and easily. Used with a light touch, the marks erase easily with a white eraser.

Washable kid's markers work surprisingly well on just about any type of fabric. We particularly like the fine-tip washable markers for detailed patterns and precise lines. However, washable in the name is not a guarantee. Be sure to test. *fig. K*

WASHABLE GLUE STICKS   We use these to glue baste our patches into place. Glue basting allows us to layer and glue as we go for fast placement. Even when we are pin basting, we like to use washable glue sticks to ensure our layered boro patches don't shift and bubble during handling and stitching. If we need to move a patch, we just pull it up, place it where we want it, and glue it back into place. Any residual glue washes right out. Oh, and don't worry about the purple ones—the color disappears in a few minutes and we haven't had it stain our fabric yet. Test your fabric if you have doubts. *fig. L*

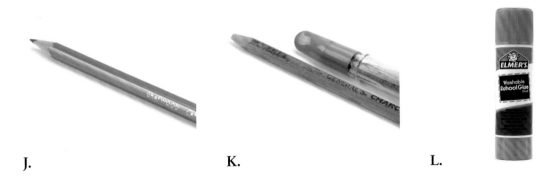

J.   **K.**   **L.**

BLOCKING MATS   Interlocking garage floor mats or exercise room mats make perfect blocking mats for pinning down fabric before we draw our lines for sashiko stitching. Resist the urge to buy the more colorful mats designed for use in children's play-rooms. We have seen unfortunate events where those pretty, pretty colors have bled onto fabric. *fig. M*

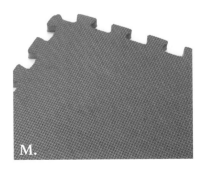

M.

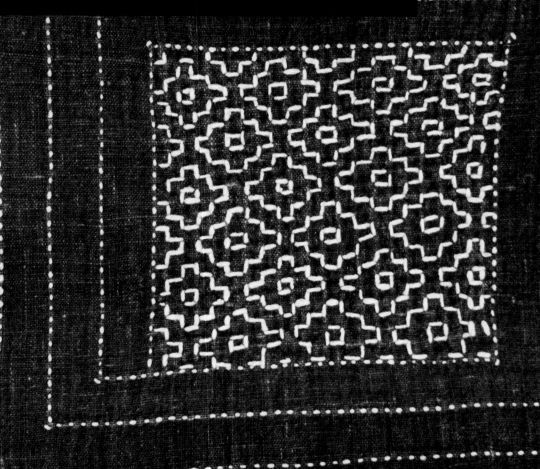

BASIC PRINCIPLES
OF SASHIKO

Running Stitch

The running stitch is the basis for all sashiko. It is the application of the running stitches that gives each of the styles of sashiko their distinctive look.

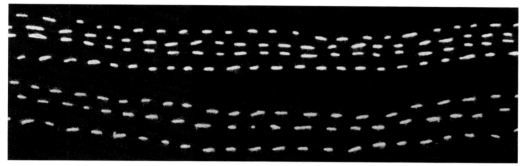

Running stitch

There are general rules about how to make the different sashiko stitches. Some of these should be followed all the time *every* time, as in hitomezashi grid patterns, but others can be adapted as the fabric dictates.

FABRIC THICKNESS

The thinner the fabric, the smaller the stitches you can make; the thicker the fabric, the larger your stitches will have to be.

When fabric is thick or you are working through multiple layers of fabric and patches, the running stitches must be longer since the needle will not bend and take smaller "bites" of the fabric as it slides along the path of your stitches. You can manipulate the fabric by lifting your fabric hand to meet the needle, but this process allows for only two or three stitches at a time since it is nearly impossible to push the needle through the thick fabric layers on the needle, even with the palm thimble. With thinner fabric, the fabric bends over the tip of the needle more easily and the slightest rocking motion with your needle hand will move the needle up and down through the fabric smoothly.

ONE STITCH PER HOLE

Sashiko stitches do not come in and out of the same holes. Other than "it's just not done that way," we have only our own speculation and the supporting evidence we found in the original pieces from the Seattle Art Museum. When we tested stitches on the same style of loosely woven fabrics as the original sashiko pieces, we found that two stitches coming through the same hole not only erased the distinctive sashiko appearance of the stitches but it also created a larger hole in the fabric. This would have been in direct opposition to one of the original intents of sashiko, which was to strengthen the fabric.

Beyond these general rules, each style of sashiko stitches has its own set of unique characteristics that makes them immediately recognizable. The two we use in this book are hitomezashi and moyouzashi. Generally, hitomezashi is made using single stitches worked on a grid and moyouzashi is made using straight or curved lines of running stitches.

Hitomezashi

Hitomezashi-style sashiko is made using running stitches worked on a grid. The size of that grid and stitch pattern determine the length of the stitches. For example, in the offset running stitch *(page 85)*, the length of both the over-stitch (the stitch on top of the fabric) and the under-stitch (the stitch under the fabric) is the distance between the intersection of the grid lines.

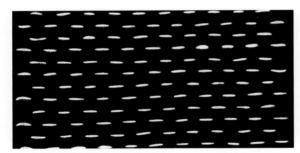

Offset running stitch over–stitches as seen from the right side of the fabric

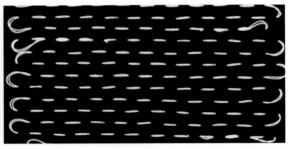

Offset running stitch under–stitches as seen from the wrong side of the fabric

Hitomezashi stitches do not curve, and the lines may cross on the top of the fabric. Since the over-stitch and the under-stitch are made according to the lines of a set grid, the stitch lengths are very precise, and the lines are very well defined. If you are having a particularly type-A day and need everything to line up in perfect little rows and columns, hitomezashi will feel very satisfying.

Hitomezashi star stitch *(page 93)* from the right side of the fabric. Note none of the stitches cross.

Hitomezashi star stitch from the wrong side of the fabric. Note the crossing stitches.

DO THIS, NOT THAT

Shannon's grandmother used to say, "If you want perfect, you'll have to use a machine. This is handwork and it's good 'nuff." She's not wrong, but she also followed rules and guidelines and would quickly fix errant stitches or techniques. We're all for breaking the rules and doing your own thing as long as you like the way the end result looks, but there are a few rules that you should follow as you create your boro and sashiko textiles. Being mindful of your stitches and honing your skills with these rules in mind will not only maintain the integrity of your textiles but will preserve the traditions of sashiko handed down through generations of stitchers.

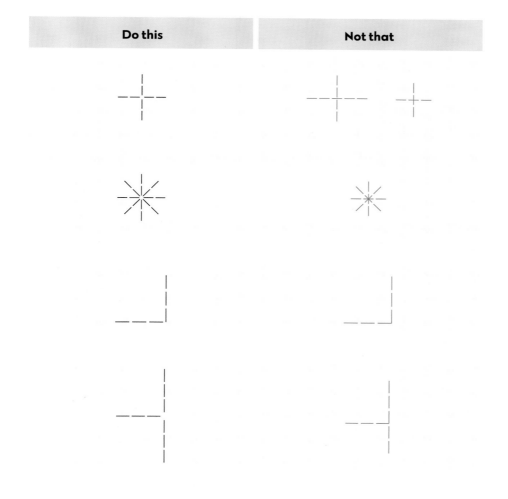

▮ Moyouzashi

Moyouzashi-style sashiko is characterized by straight or curved lines of running stitches that do not cross on top of the fabric. Moyouzashi running stitches are worked on patterns drawn out using grids or the outline of a picture or symbol. Moyouzashi running stitches also lend themselves beautifully to random or abstract lines.

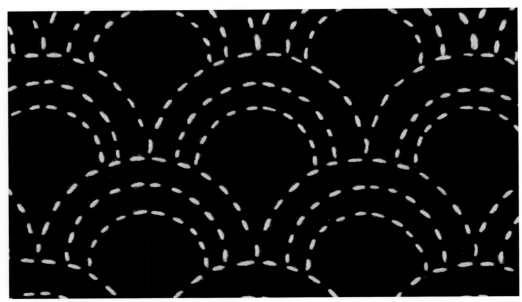

Moyouzashi stitches in the wave pattern *(page 97)* on a grid

Moyouzashi running stitches in an abstract pattern

In moyouzashi, the size of your stitches will depend entirely on the thickness of the fabric and the size of the overall pattern. Generally, we aim for moyouzashi to be made with a 2:1 stitch-length ratio. This means the over-stitch is twice as long as the under-stitch.

The over-stitch of moyouzashi is twice as long as the under-stitch.

When you work very small patterns or lines of a pattern that are drawn very close together, the details of the design will stand out better in smaller stitches. In these cases, the 2:1 stitch-length ratio becomes closer to a 1:1 stitch-length ratio to prevent pulling the fabric threads too much as the sashiko needle and thread are pulled through the fabric.

Tip: Push and Pull

If you are working through heavy or dense fabric (denim, canvas) or a few layers of fabric, you might have to push the needle and pull the fabric off the needle more frequently.

Choosing Your Stitches

The density of the fabric you are stitching will determine the style and pattern of your sashiko stitches. If you are stitching over patches of fabric that fray easily, you will need to work more stitches, or a denser stitch pattern, over the patches to keep the edges from fraying excessively. That said, a certain amount of fraying on raw-edge patches is expected and even exactly what you might want! Choose the stitch pattern and the density of the stitches so the fabric patch is stitched down enough so no large sections of edging are free and likely to be caught and torn.

COMBINING FABRICS: AESTHETICS AND FUNCTION

A pack of fabrics from the Cotton Couture collection from Michael Miller Fabrics, used in the Lotus Pond Throw (*page 144*)

Historical pieces of boro and sashiko are richly layered textiles that were created out of the necessity to repair and strengthen the rough, plant-based, loosely woven fabrics available to the Japanese people of the time. The climate was harsh, as were the laws about wearing fabrics made from better materials, so they made do with what they had.

Even these intrepid researchers found it difficult to find a modern equivalent to this rustic fabric. The present-day maker has a comparatively extravagant choice of fabrics made from a nearly endless variety of materials created in fine gauze to heavy canvases and everything in between. No longer are we creating boro textiles out of necessity or dire need but out of respect for the craft and for our own enjoyment. Now we can create with the fabric first and foremost in our mind, since our materials are easily customized to match our needed outcome—the finished project—rather than making do with that we have at hand.

If You Can Stitch on It, You Can Use It!

We have used cottons, silks, and synthetics of all types for both the base and scrap fabric to make boro textiles. As long as the stitches stand out against the surface of the fabric and don't get lost in a long-nap fabric such as faux fur or other fuzzy novelty fabric, you can work with it for creating boro-style textiles.

A pile of scraps ready for use

The real key is to be aware that you are creating a whole new textile when you are adding patches, layers, and stitching. The final fabric will not have the same drape, texture, and strength of the individual fabrics. You can even use a muslin or canvas (watch for sales ... we keep bolts of the stuff around) and completely change the nature of those less-expensive fabrics into something with stunning complexity. After layering of patches and stitching is complete, the new composite fabric you have created is greater than the sum of its parts, taking on new and often surprising qualities. This added layer of delightful discovery is one of the elements that drives us with an almost obsessive fervor to create more boro and sashiko textiles ... often whether we have a project in mind for them or not!

Fabric-First Design

Creating fabric first is thinking first about the composite textile we are making while keeping a thought to the context of the final project. When creating a new piece, we can start with any base we want and build on that. We can create the textile first with the form and function of the end product in mind and make our decisions about fabric, density of patches, and stitches in that context. How much drape and movement do we want or how sturdy should the new fabric be in order to hold up to wear? Without considering the form and function, we can get carried away (as one does in creative endeavors) and make some serious errors in fabric and stitching choice.

FORM AND FUNCTION

When putting together composite textiles, you can certainly use any mix of fabric types that makes you happy, but you should always consider the use and purpose of the finished piece. Your final decisions have to reflect what you are going to make from the materials as well as how it is going to be used in the real world.

A tote bag made from vintage kimono scraps will look *fab* being carried around town but won't exactly be the best choice for carrying produce home from the grocery store. Live in a warm climate? Go easy on the patches and go heavy on the stitching to keep your final fabric lighter and more breathable. Likewise, if the finished piece is going to undergo heavy wear and tear, the stitch pattern should use smaller stitches so no unfortunate snags occur. We have a denim jacket covered in boro and sashiko that is in heavy rotation in our wardrobe. We knew this was going to be the case, so all of the stitches are short so we don't catch the threads and pull or break them.

Selecting fabrics for our Reversible Knot Bag *(page 108)*, which has lots of boro patches and sashiko stitching, with the stitches fairly small to stand up to wear

▌ KEEP IT CLEAN

Remember, when you are patching together "random" pieces of scrap fabric from modern sources—your closet, thrift stores, vintage clothes, that bag (or two) of old clothes in the crawl space above your studio (What? You don't have a bag of don't-throw-that-out-we-might-be-able-to-use-that clothes?)—you are creating a new composite fabric that must be treated according to how you would treat the most delicate of the fabric in your piece.

You might have a garment that is predominantly cotton, but you've also pieced in some delicious wool and silk scraps. The cotton will be just fine in the regular wash, but the wool and silk will not react so nicely. For this purpose, we either decide the heck with it and wash everything before piecing, or just know that we can never throw that particular finished piece in the regular wash cycle.

So, yes, experiment and play with fabrics. But always consider your final composite fabric and how it will be used. If you are making a throw that will see heavy use by family members (human and nonhuman), you probably want to use mostly durable and wash-able fabrics. On the other hand, a wallhanging that will act as a piece of art can include more delicate fabrics like silk. Special garments that you or the recipient are willing to hand-wash and will wear gently are the perfect place to use those vintage or more delicate fabrics.

Tip: Three Beans Bin

"If you can wrap three beans in a piece of cloth, then it is big enough to keep." —Japanese idiom

"Hey! Don't throw that out ... we might be able to use it!" —The authors

This Japanese saying spoke to us because we keep pieces of fabric of every shape and size in scrap bins by every workspace "just in case." We even come home from teaching and empty our jacket pockets and luggage of scraps we created or that were left behind. You never know when that perfect piece of fabric is going to come along again ... so save them all just in case.

Color, Fabric, and Stitches

After how to make the stitches, the questions we are most frequently asked are how we decide on colors and how to place patches and stitching. This is the point where you might expect us to go into detail about color theory and composition, discussing values and weight and complementary and adjacent and … no.

The best way to make color choices is to pick out your favorite colors and put them together in a way that makes you happy. Sure, if you get stuck, you can grab a color wheel and do a quick reference to spark some creativity. Nothing wrong with that! We have been known to use a color wheel when all of the color choices start to swim before our eyes.

However, equally valuable is a trip to your closet or living room or a look at the ads in a magazine. See those colors in your closet? How do you put together an outfit for the day? How about those colors in your living room? How do the curtains work with the carpet, pillows, and furniture? That's all color theory in practical application.

The same is true of the placement of large pieces of fabric and smaller patches in these projects. We have provided diagrams that show where we put the patches and where we put sashiko patterns, but if you want to add or take away, go for it! Especially with boro and sashiko, you will develop your own sense of style in regard to placement and design pieces.

There is one additional non-aesthetic decision about fabric and stitch placement that should not be overlooked. If you are layering fabrics, you will need to use less dense fabric for your backing/base fabric to make it easier to push the needle through all the layers. If you want to use a fairly simple, large running stitch, denser layers are okay. But if you are trying to make a more delicate or intricate stitch pattern, thick layers will not allow that.

So you have two goals for your new composite fabric—that it be aesthetically pleasing and that it is suited for the project's use. Will the garment fabric have enough drape and movement? Will my tote bag be strong enough? Can I wear this garment in my climate?

Create and take chances! You can always take out or add stitches and move, remove, and add patches—we certainly do this *a lot*. But always create your composite textiles with a mindful eye toward the end goal of your project.

▌ PLACEMENT OF PATCHES

Through the study of countless boro blankets, futon covers, garments, and textile fragments, we have come up with a system by which we emulate the random nature of boro.

What initially starts as one large piece of fabric begins breaking up through the addition of only slightly smaller fabric panels that cover large areas of the original fabric. This was often due to wear and tear from repeated use in working conditions—such as a harness or strap for pulling a cart or boat—or from repeated use in the home, such as a much-used futon cover or garment. Finally, layers of smaller patches are placed in juxtaposition to one another and to the larger patches, then stitched over to "lock down" the overlapping edges of the patches, making the resulting composite fabric stronger.

Tip: From a Distance

The best way to decide if you like the placement of your patches is to stand back and look at them from a distance. Quilters typically do this by putting their intended creation up on a design wall where they can stand across the room and see if they are ready to make their work permanent.

If, like us, you are a bit more space challenged, you might not have the luxury of an entire wall for perspective. Instead, we stand over our proposed patchwork piece and take a photo with our mobile device. Then, we look at the photo either on that device or on a computer. We often do this several times until we are completely happy and are ready for the proposed to become permanent.

GETTING READY
TO STITCH

Threading the Needle

Sashiko thread is held double; the thickness makes the stitches stand out against the fabric. Thread the folded end of the thread into the needle to make stops and starts easier—this allows you to remove the needle from the thread and put it aside. It makes evening out the thread over the length of the row of stitches easier as well.

1. Measure the length of the thread you will need by pulling enough thread off your spool to lay it across the line(s) you are stitching plus a small amount for turning rows, backstitching, knots, and weaving in ends. *fig. A*

2. Double the amount of thread you just measured. Remember, you are holding the thread double.

3. Fold the length of thread in half by matching up the cut ends of the thread and pinching the folded end.

4. Insert the folded end of the thread into the eye of the sashiko needle. *fig. B*

5. Leave a length of thread overlapped to keep the thread from coming out of the eye of the needle as you are making stitches. *fig. C*

A.

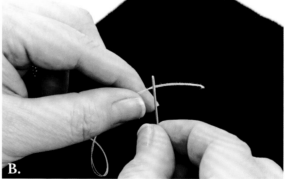

B.

C.

Drawing a True Grid

All hitomezashi stitch patterns and quite a few moyouzashi stitch patterns follow grids, so learning to draw a true grid is the key to executing beautiful lines of sashiko. We have tested many methods of laying out a grid on the surface of our fabric. Here are the three we found to be the most effective.

JUST A QUILTING RULER

If you have a see-through quilting ruler with easy-to-see guidelines, your marking process will go much more smoothly than trying to use a traditional ruler that you cannot see through.

1. Decide where your first line will be and lay the ruler along that line. Square up the other lines on the ruler to the edge of your patch or project to ensure your drawn lines are square relative to the patch or project. *fig. D*

2. With a disappearing fabric marker, draw the first line along the edge of the ruler. Brace your hands in a tented form rather than flat palmed to prevent the ruler from slipping on the fabric. *fig. E*

3. Use the measurement guides on the ruler to line up the next line with the line you have just drawn. Draw the next line. *fig. F*

4. Repeat Step 3 until the fabric or patch is filled. *fig. G*

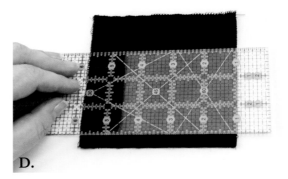

D.

E.

F.

G.

5. Move the ruler to the end of the drawn lines so it lies 90° across them. Draw your first line. *fig. H*

6. Repeat Step 3, lining up the ruler edge and guide lines with the last lines drawn, until you have a completed grid. *fig. I*

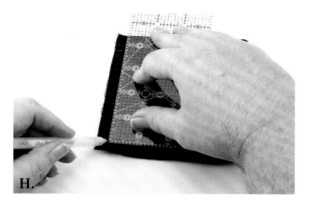

H.

I.

▌ JUST DOTS

Using your marking pen to fill in the holes of a plastic canvas grid makes a perfect grid.

1. Lay the fabric on a blocking mat and place the grid squarely on top of the fabric. *fig. J*

Tip: Pinning Down the Fabric

When we are using just a ruler, we will also pin the fabric down if we are working on large sections of fabric to prevent it from shifting.

2. Pin into place through both the grid and fabric into the blocking mat. This keeps your fabric from shifting as you draw. *fig. K*

J.

K.

3. Run your disappearing fabric marker around the inside of the grid holes to make dots on the fabric. *fig. L*

4. When you are finished, you will have a perfect dot grid! *fig. M*

L.

M.

Tip: Covering a Large Area

To cover a large area of fabric, move the plastic canvas grid to the next position on the fabric, lining up a few rows of dots to make sure your new grid placement is square with the existing dots you just drew.

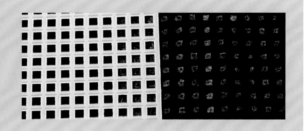

▌ DOT AND RULER

For larger areas, we have found using a combination of ruler and plastic grid dots to be the most effective and much faster than drawing dots alone. With this method, we draw the dots around the edge of the area to be filled with grid, then use the ruler to draw lines using the dots as lines.

1. Lay the plastic canvas over the fabric on the blocking mat and pin into place. Line up the holes of the plastic canvas with the edge of the area you need to fill with a grid. Fill in only the dots along the edge of the area to be filled. *fig. N*

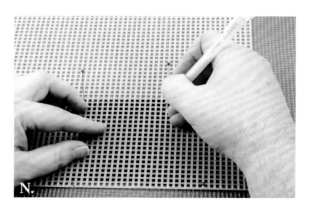

N.

2. Move the plastic grid as needed until the entire area is outlined with evenly spaced dots. As you move the grid, be sure the dots on opposite sides of the area you are marking line up, or your finished lines will not be straight. *fig. O*

3. Use your ruler to connect the dots, and draw lines with the disappearing marker. Be careful to ensure your ruler is connecting dots that are exactly opposite one another, or your lines will not be aligned properly. We like to use markers that disappear with heat so we can use a small iron to erase lines that are wrong. Yup … we do it, too! *fig. P*

4. When you are finished you will have a perfect grid! *fig. Q*

Tip: Lots of Ground to Cover!

When we have a large area to cover with grid that is oddly shaped or longer than our ruler (as is the case with the collars of the two jackets), we use the dot-and-ruler method and make an extra line of dots in the middle of the area to make lining up our ruler easier. The extra line of dots is closer together than the length of our quilting ruler, so we can draw one set of lines between the first dots and then draw a second set of lines between the next set of dots.

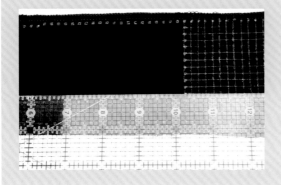

O.

P.

Q.

After your initial grid is drawn, you can draw diagonals or curves or lay other templates on the grid to line up your overall design. You also can draw in your actual stitching lines. Jason can always visualize his stitch line for persimmon flower *(page 90)* without following a pattern, but Shannon always draws in the first few stitch guide lines or he invariably makes one of the variations. Which is fine ... it's totally fine ... unless you had your heart set on the persimmon flower, in which case ... *Gah!*

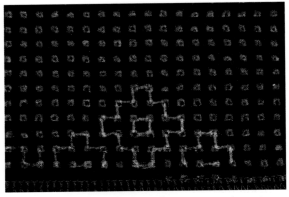

Stitching lines for the persimmon flower pattern drawn into the grid

Tip: Other Grids

Not every pattern is stitched on a 1:1 grid. You will see some are worked on a 2:1 grid or even a 3:1 grid. You can adjust the dots or lines you draw using your plastic canvas grid to accommodate these different grid ratios ahead of time, or you can simply draw in the stitching lines after the 1:1 grid is completed.

Drawing Other Shapes

FOLLOWING A TEMPLATE

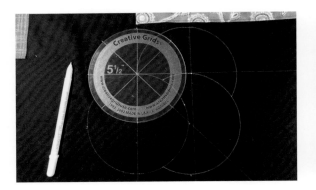

If you can lay it on your fabric and outline or trace it, you can use it as a marking template. We use plastic canvas grids in circles and triangles to drawn concentric shapes. We also have used wine glasses, soup cans, cookie cutters, and quilting templates. For large areas or more complex patterns, pin your fabric into place before using the template.

FREEHAND LINES

Shannon drawing lines on the yoke of his chambray shirt

▊ To Knot or Not?

Whether to knot or not largely depends on the fabric you are working with and the function of the piece you are making. For example, a garment where the threads could work loose over time might require knots to start and stop your thread lines. We saw numerous examples of this in the historical pieces we studied. Here we offer both knotted and knotless stops and starts as well as an alternative to knots that comes from our hand-sewing and quilting backgrounds. Use them at your discretion depending on the fabric, stitch pattern, and the form and function of the piece you are making.

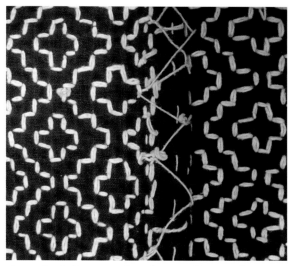

The inside of a kimono in the collection of the Seattle Art Museum, showing knots at the end of the stitching lines

▊ KNOTTED STARTS AND STOPS

When you make your first stitches in Unshin Exercise #1 *(page 58)*, we tell you to use knots until you have mastered handling the needle, fabric, and thimble, and making stitches. Knots are necessary for garments where wear and use could cause the thread tails to come undone. Knots also come in handy in fabrics with stretch, such as stretch denim, where the threads can work themselves loose.

▊ A TALE OF TWO KNOTS

There are two types of knots and both work equally well. Jason was taught one method and Shannon the other, so while they have both learned the other's version of making a knot, they still hold steadfast because that's how they've always done it. One is not better than the other. No, really—it's fine either way (really!). Don't worry. We won't ask you to take sides.

Needle Knot

Also known as "the quilter's knot," as taught to Jason by his mother.

1. Hold the threaded needle with the tip pointed out and lay the cut end of the thread across the shaft. *fig. R*

R.

2. Hold the thread securely across the shaft of the needle with your thumb. *fig. S*

S.

3. Wrap the thread around the needle 4–5 times. The more wraps, the larger your knot will be. *fig. T*

T.

4. Hold the wrapped thread firmly with 2 fingers while pushing the needle through the wrap. *fig. U*

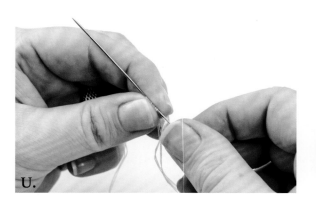

U.

5. Keep a firm pinch on the wrapped thread as you pull the thread all the way through until it is snug. *Ta-da!* A knot! *fig. V*

V.

Spit Knot

Also known as "the quilter's knot," as taught to Shannon by his grandmother.

1. Wet your index finger (that's the spit part). If we've lost you here, see the Needle Knot instructions *(page 47)*. Otherwise, read on.

2. Lay the cut end of the thread across your finger and make one wrap over the cut end to hold it in place. *fig. W*

3. Use your thumb to roll the thread off your index finger. You should see the thread coil around itself. Stop at 3 or 4 coils. *fig. X*

4. Pinch the coiled thread between your thumb and index finger and pull the thread tight. *fig. Y*

Ta-da! Another knot that's just as good as the other one. Just. As. Good.

Starting with a Knot—No Layers

Whichever of the knots you chose to make, you are now ready to stitch. Simply set your knot as instructed in Unshin Exercise #1 *(page 58)* and you're on your way. When working through one layer of fabric like this, the knots will obviously show on the back of the fabric.

Starting with a Knot—Layers

If you are working through layers of fabric, you can pop your knot to hide it between layers.

1. First make your knot; then insert your needle between the layers of the fabric, sliding it along for a few inches. Bring your needle out where you want your first stitch to start.

2. Pull the thread through until the knot catches on the fabric, then gently tug on the thread while holding the fabric next to the knot. The knot will pop through the fabric and will now be hidden between the layers of fabric.

This takes a bit of practice and the knot has to be just the right size—too large and it will not pop through the fabric without leaving a hole, too small and it will slip out of the fabric at the place where you make your first stitch.

Ending with a Knot—Layers / No Layers

To end with a knot, backtrack your stitches on the back of your fabric. Either make a needle knot *(page 47)* at the end or make a knot around one of the back stitches. If you are working with layers, run the needle between the layers of fabric for a few inches, bring the needle up through the fabric, and trim the end.

Knotless Start—No Layers

A knotless start requires working a few stitches in the opposite direction of your intended stitching row. This means you will need to eyeball where the first few stitches of your row are going to go. When we first started making the knotless start, we would stitch the first few stitches with the needle then pull it out of the fabric, leaving only the marks for the stitches. Then we would follow those stitch marks backward.

Needle marks in the fabric showing the path for the first few stitches to follow when making a knotless start

Being able to guesstimate the placement of these first few backward stitches will be easier the more stitches you make.

1. Make 3 or 4 stitches in the opposite direction of your intended line of stitches. *fig. Z*

2. When you are one stitch from where you will begin your line of stitches, bring your needle up at the start of the line, preparing to make a back stitch. *fig. AA*

3. Turn your work and insert your needle back into the fabric in the direction of your stitching line to complete the first stitch. *fig. BB*

Turn your work over to ensure your needle is coming out between the 2 strands of the under-stitch threads on the underside of your fabric. *fig. CC*

Be careful not to split any one strand of the thread with the tip of the needle. If you miss the 2 strands, use the eye of the needle to bring the working thread up between the 2 strands of the under-stitch. *fig. DD*

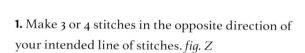

4. With the back of your work facing you, make a few shadow stitches by carefully slipping your needle under the fabric beneath the next 3 or 4 over-stitches. If you are working on a layered fabric, slip the needle under only 1 layer of fabric. *fig. EE*

Be very careful here to not push the needle through the threads of the over-stitches, or you will end up with gnarled-looking stitches on the surface of your work. A little patience goes a long way for a beautiful row of stitches on the surface of your work.

5. Once you have made a few shadow stitches, turn your work over and bring the tip of the needle up to start the next stitch. *fig. FF*

6. Continue with your line of stitching. When you are finished with the row, trim off the tail of the starting thread. *fig. GG*

Tip: Check That Tail
We have found it adds to our peace of mind to add a small dot of a product like Fray Check to secure the end of the thread tail.

Knotless Start—Layers
If you are working with layers of fabric, first run your needle between the layers of fabric for a few inches and bring the tip of the needle out where you want to make your first stitches. Pull the thread through until 2″–3″ of thread remain. Trim the tail when the row of stitches is complete.

EE.

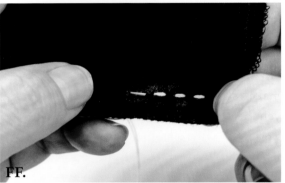

FF.

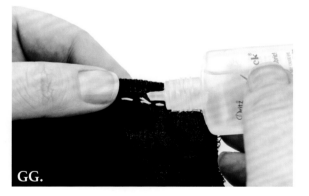

GG.

Knotless Ending—With or Without Layers

1. When you are 1 stitch from where you will end your line of stitches, bring the needle up at the end of the line, preparing to make a back stitch. *fig. HH*

2. Turn your work. Insert your needle back into the fabric against the line of your stitching to complete the last stitch. *fig. II*

Turn your work over to make sure the needle is coming out between the 2 strands of the under-stitch threads. *fig. JJ*

3. With the back of your work facing you, make 2 shadow stitches by carefully slipping your needle under the fabric beneath the next 2 over-stitches. If you are working on a layered fabric, slip the needle under only 1 layer of fabric. *fig. KK*

HH.

II.

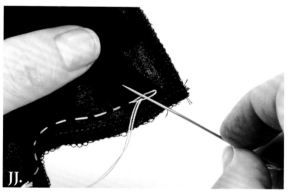
JJ.

KK.

4. If you are working through only 1 layer of fabric, leave a small tail and clip your thread. This is where that little dot of Fray Check can add peace of mind if you are afraid your thread might still slip loose. Or you can opt for a knotted ending. *fig. LL*

If you are working through layers of fabric, slip the needle between the layers of fabric for a few inches and trim just as you did for a knotless start.

▌KNOTLESS ALTERNATIVE

We have worked with a few fabrics in which we did not want to make a visible knot but that left us less than confident that our knotless starts and stops would hold with wear and tear. For those, we borrowed from our hand-quilting and sewing backgrounds and worked an anchor stitch at the beginning and end of our rows.

1. Start just as you would for a knotless start or ending. After making 1 or 2 shadow stitches, make a stitch back around the fabric your last shadow stitch just went under. *fig. MM*

2. Do this one more time. Be careful not to push your needle through the threads on the surface of the fabric to prevent a gnarled-looking over-stitch. *figs. NN-OO*

3. Continue on with your start just as you normally would, or trim the tail for an ending.

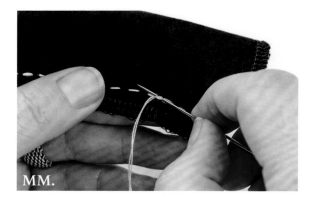

An anchor stitch from the bottom of the fabric.

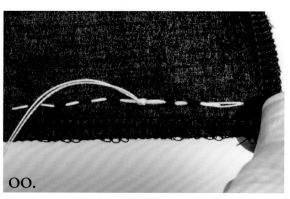

An anchor stitch from the top of the fabric.

Basting Three Ways

When it all comes down to it, sashiko is quilting without a frame. We put together layers of fabric and build up more layers with boro patches; then we stitch over them to hold everything in place and to strengthen the overall fabric. To keep those layers from sliding around, resulting in large bubbles and puckers, baste the layers together using thread, pins, or glue ... or even a combination of those!

THREAD BASTING can be done by hand or with a sewing machine. Our BERNINA B 790 PLUS has a basting stitch setting that we put to good use on larger patches, such as those in the throw and the wallhanging. A quick baste around the edges of the turned appliqué patches made them behave during the hand stitching around the edges. The same can be done on the large open areas of fabric on the wallhanging and throw to keep the layers of fabric from sliding around during stitching, leaving bubbles of fabric that don't line up correctly.

PIN BASTING can be done with regular straight pins or, our preference, coiless safety pins. Basting with coiless safety pins prevents turning yourself into a pincushion while handling a piece during stitching. Plus they don't slip out.

GLUE BASTING is our go-to. As we said in The Tools (*page 22*), washable glue sticks are a must for our studio and we buy them in bulk. A quick glue baste will even help hold larger pieces of fabric in place while you pin baste with the coiless safety pins. We did this combo baste with the throw, wrap vest, and wallhanging projects.

Baste, baste, baste! The more you baste, the less slippage you will have in your fabric so you don't end up with a lot of loose baggy spots and ripples to ease in.

Tip: The Pat Down

Despite best efforts to evenly baste fabric layers, you will still encounter bubbles in the fabric as you stitch. Bubbles occur when one layer of fabric is larger than the underlying fabric. Even small discrepancies in the two layers can result in a bubble. Careful basting will significantly reduce the occurrence of bubbles, but they can still pop up with the handling of the fabric for stitching. To get rid of bubbles, we ease them back in with a good pat down. With the project laying on a flat surface, start at the center of the bubble and pat the fabric down, working your hands outward until the fabric is even distributed over the affected area. Do not smooth or slide your hands over the fabric but continue to pat down until you are satisfied. Now get out your coiless safety pins and pin the area into place.

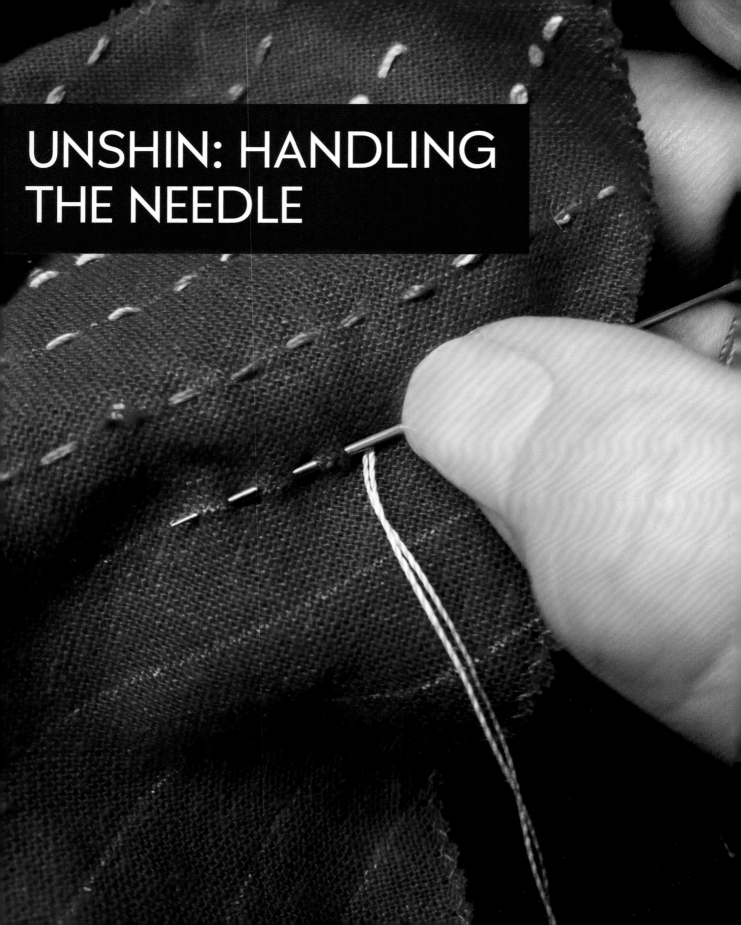

UNSHIN: HANDLING THE NEEDLE

And now it's time for the *real* reason y'all bought this book ... making stitches and pretty fabrics! At the heart of boro and sashiko is the sashiko needle. Learning to properly handle the distinctive needle and thimble used to manipulate the thread through the fabric is the first step on the slippery slope to boro and sashiko obsession.

To that end, we use two exercises for our introductory classes to learn *unshin*, which means "handling the needle." The running stitch is something you can intellectually understand, but it is only the exercise of putting needle to fabric using the unique palm thimble and rocker motion of sashiko that will make you proficient at this awe-inspiring stitching skill.

Here is a list of basic materials and tools; see The Tools *(page 22)* for more details.

FABRIC PIECES   We usually start folx out on a swatch at least 6″ × 6″ (15.2 × 15.2 cm). A plain piece of quilting cotton or even a scrap of an old cotton shirt is perfect for practicing.

THREAD   We recommend Aurifil 12-weight thread for these exercises. It is an excellent weight for sashiko when held double and is much smoother than other thread available from retailers or online.

SASHIKO NEEDLE

SASHIKO PALM THIMBLE

THREAD SNIPS

Terminology

TOP SIDE AND BACK SIDE

The top side of the fabric is the side that will show on the outside of your finished projects. The back side of the fabric is where your knots, loops, and woven-in ends will be.

NEEDLE HAND AND FABRIC HAND

Whether you are left-hand or right-hand dominant, your needle hand will be the hand you use to hold the needle. The opposite hand will be the fabric hand, which feeds the fabric toward the point of the needle.

▎NEEDLE HAND

The needle hand maneuvers the needle along the path of the stitching line and also pulls the fabric onto the needle as it moves through the fabric. The middle finger and thumb of the needle hand perform the up-and-down rocking motion of the running stitches. Along with the fabric hand, the needle hand maintains the tension of the fabric to make the movement of the needle easier. Loose fabric makes it difficult to move the tip of the needle through the fabric. The more taut the fabric, the easier the stitches are to make.

The needle hand is also where you will wear the palm thimble. The palm thimble both braces the needle against the divots in the metal and gently pushes the needle forward as you rock it up and down to make the stitches.

▎FABRIC HAND

The fabric hand holds the side of the fabric that you have not stitched into yet and feeds that fabric toward the tip of the needle. The fabric hand also wiggles the unworked fabric up and down over the tip of the needle, mirroring the up-and-down rocking movement of the needle. Along with the needle hand, the fabric hand maintains the tension of the fabric.

▎Unshin Exercise #1

▎MOYOUZASHI RUNNING STITCH

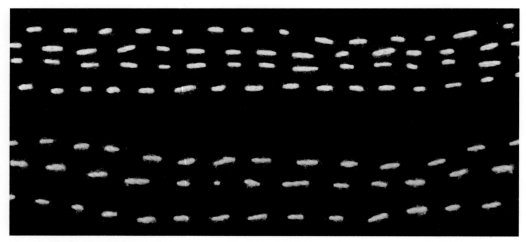

Moyouzashi running stitch swatch

For this exercise, you are going to make a freehand stitch without any guidelines or grid marks. The first time through, you will not be expected to make perfectly spaced moyouzashi stitches at a 2:1 stitch-length ratio. Remember, this exercise is solely for the purpose of learning to handle the sashiko needle. It will take practice for you to develop a rhythm with your needle that allows you to achieve more evenly spaced running stitches.

While this is a necessary practice and must be done to achieve proper needle-handling techniques, these first practice patches are often the most beautiful since they are raw and unre-fined and truly random. We still have our very first practice pieces and, at the time of the writing of this sentence, still haven't found suitably special projects to mount them onto—not yet.

Our very first practice swatches with moyouzashi stitches

1. Thread the needle as shown in Threading the Needle *(page 41).*

2. Place the palm thimble on your middle finger. *fig. A*

3. Make a knot *(page 47).*

4. Coming from the back of the fabric, insert the needle about ¼″ to ½″ (0.6 to 1.2 cm) from the edge. Pull the thread through to set the knot. (For now, we are using knots to start this exercise. As you become more proficient, practice the knotless start and stops from To Knot or Not?*, page 47.*) *fig. B*

5. Brace the end of the sashiko needle with the eye against the palm thimble, using the little dimples in the metal to secure the end of the needle and keep it from slipping around. *fig. C*

6. Place your middle finger beneath the fabric, under the needle. *fig. D*

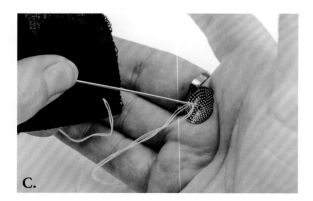

C.

D.

7. Place your thumb on the top of the needle over the fabric. *fig. E*

You now have the needle braced in 3 places (*fig. F*):

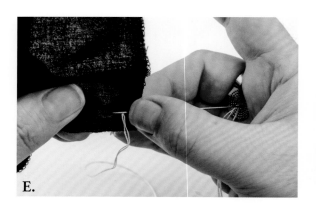

E.

F.

The eye of the sashiko needle is braced against the dimples of the palm thimble, with the thumb and middle finger pinching the needle to the fabric.

8. Gather the fabric with your opposite hand. *fig. G*

Remember, you will keep the tension on the fabric between your 2 hands to make the needle move more easily through the fabric. This tension with your hands takes the place of an embroidery hoop or a stretcher frame. As you pull the fabric onto your needle with one hand, you will slowly release fabric from your opposite hand and feed that fabric toward the needle. One hand feeds, the other pulls onto the needle. Don't worry—the execution of this becomes immediately automatic as you start making stitches, and you won't be thinking about it much at all.

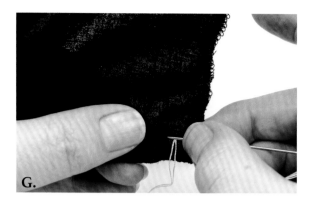

G.

Note: Overview of the Next Few Steps

Now you will rock the needle up and down while pulling the fabric onto the needle with your middle finger and thumb. This is not a large movement! Since you are making stitches through a single layer of lightweight fabric, the rocker motion of the needle does not need to be very big in order to move the tip of the needle over and under the surface of the fabric.

At the same time, you will gently push the needle through the fabric with the palm thimble. This is accomplished with a slight squeezing motion as your middle finger and thumb pull the fabric onto the needle and toward the palm of your hand.

9. With your needle hand, rock the needle down so the tip is below the fabric. Gently push the needle forward with the palm thimble. Use a very small movement with your fabric hand to lift the fabric slightly to meet the tip of the needle. *fig. H*

H.

10. With your needle hand, rock the needle up so the tip is above the fabric. Continue to gently push the needle forward with the palm thimble. Use a very small movement with your fabric hand to push the fabric down slightly to meet the tip of the needle. *fig. I*

I.

11. Continue to rock the needle up then down as in Steps 9 and 10, loading more fabric onto your needle. *fig. J*

As you make more stitches, use a very small movement to pull the worked fabric onto the needle. You will pull the worked fabric only as far as you need to make the needle point go into the fabric a short distance from where it came up.

J.

Take your time to learn the rhythm and feel of moving the needle and fabric together. You are performing 3 coordinated movements: rock the needle, pull and feed the fabric, and wiggle the feeding fabric up and down to enhance the movement and efficiency of the movement of the needle hand. This overall handling of the needle to make running stitches is unshin and takes practice to solidify as a natural movement.

12. When you come to the end of your row (or the end of your fabric), finish your line of stitches with your needle point under the fabric. Remember to leave about ¼″ to ½″ (0.6 to 1.2 cm) of unworked fabric at the edges of your swatch. If you run stitches right up to the edge of the fabric, it will tend to pucker and pull too easily.

You will have a handful of fabric in your needle hand. This fabric is bunched up on the needle like the gathers of a curtain when they are pulled open ... just a little messier. This is where the true power of your palm thimble comes into play.

13. Brace your needle against the palm thimble, and hold the gathered fabric near the tip of the needle in place with the thumb and middle finger of your fabric hand. Make sure your grip is firm enough to hold the fabric in place but loose enough to allow the needle to slide through your fingers. With the palm thimble, push the needle as far as possible through the gathered fabric. *fig. K*

K.

14. Grab the gathered fabric again with your fabric hand by pinching the gathered fabric against the needle at the point where the needle tip comes out of the fabric. This will keep the gathered fabric from exploding off the tip of the needle. *fig. L*

15. With your needle hand, pull the fabric across the length of the thread while securely holding the needle with your fabric hand. *fig. M*

L.

Tip: When Push Comes to Shove

If the fabric just won't come off the needle over the thread, push the eye of the needle again with your palm thimble until you can pull more fabric free. Thick fabric and dense layers will cause this to happen most often, but even the thinnest fabric can tighten up on the needle if too much is loaded onto the needle. On the next set of stitches you make, put fewer stitches into the fabric before pushing and pulling through.

M.

16. With your needle hand, pinch the fabric along with the knot end of the thread and gently run your fabric hand along the length of the thread (from the knot end to the needle end) to redistribute the fabric evenly. *fig. N*

N.

17. While still pinching the fabric and knot end of the thread with your needle hand, give the fabric at the end of the row a gentle pull with your fabric hand to give a final check for evening out the stitches. This should cause a number of the stitches to pop up on the surface of the fabric. *fig. O*

18. Now, still pinching the fabric and knot end of the thread with your needle hand, gently pull on the needle end of the thread with your fabric hand until the stitches even out and lay neatly along the length of the fabric. Your goal is to have no stitches popped up above the surface of the fabric. *fig. P*

First row made. ... *Ta-da!* Bask in your skills and take a deep breath. Here comes the second row!

19. With the top side of your fabric facing you, rotate your work 180° so your needle is again on the needle-hand side. *fig. Q*

20. Push the tip of your needle from the back to the top of the fabric and pull the thread through ... *fig. R*

21. ... until a small loop of thread remains on the back of the fabric. This safety loop is essential to maintain proper tension between the thread and fabric. Leave a larger loop when you first start. You can adjust the size of the safety loop when you come to the end of your row and smooth the fabric over the length of the thread. Failure to leave a safety loop will result in an extremely tight pucker that will be difficult to even out. In the case of garments and larger projects, this pucker can worsen with wear and use. Always leave a safety loop! *fig. S*

S.

22. Repeat Steps 5–15. *fig. T*

23. As you did in Step 16, pinch the fabric with your needle hand, but now include the loop you left at the beginning of the row rather than the knot (the loop is now where the knot was in the previous row).

T.

24. Still pinching the fabric and loop end of the thread with your needle hand, gently pull on the needle end of the thread with your fabric hand until the stitches even out and lie neatly along the length of the fabric. As was the case in Step 20, your goal is to have no stitches popped up above the surface of the fabric. *fig. U*

U.

Tip: The Goldilocks Loop Zone

Keep an eye on your safety loop here! The safety loop should shrink slightly without tightening flush against the back of the fabric. If it is too tight, use the eye end of your needle to maneuver the thread along the path of your stitches until the loop is looser. If it is too loose, hold the fabric next to the loop with your fabric hand and gently pull on the needle end of the thread until the safety loop just the right size to give your fabric enough give to prevent puckers with wear and use.

Too big

Too small

Just right!

Second row finished! *Woo-hoo!* Now repeat Steps 19–24 for a few more rows. With each row, remind yourself of The Stitcher's Promise *(page 11)*, and gently evaluate whether you need to even out the distance between your stitches or lengthen or shorten your over-stitches. The more rows you make, the more consistent your stitches will become and the more ease you will feel when making your stitches.

▌ NEXT STITCHES

After a couple of rows, when you feel like you are starting to have the basic rocker motion under control, use a ruler and a marking pen to mark out some straight lines to follow. See if you can maintain stitch evenness and follow a line.

Unshin Exercise #2

▍HITOMEZASHI OFFSET RUNNING STITCH

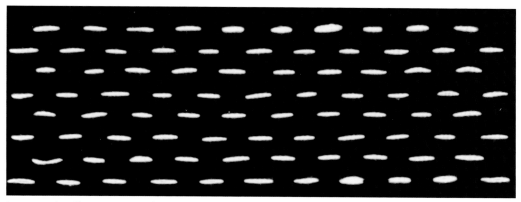

Hitomezashi offset running stitches swatch

Now let's add a little more structure with a grid, à la hitomezashi offset running stitches. Remember that hitomezashi stitches are worked on a grid, and the size of the grid and the stitch pattern determine the length of the stitches. There is no guesswork as to the size of the over- or under-stitches. Just follow the grid … the grid rules all in hitomezashi! For practice, we suggest you draw a grid with lines about ¼″ (6 mm) apart.

The offset running stitch in this second exercise is the basis for a profusion of other hitomezashi patterns, and it makes a great stand-alone stitch for fastening down patches for layered patchwork and visible mending patches. This is the first stitch most folx learn to eyeball and make comfortably without the use of a drawn grid.

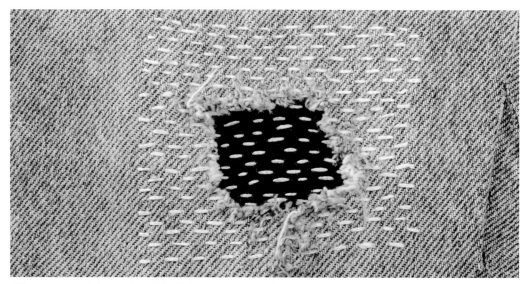

Offset running stitches make a *fab* stitch for visible mending patches.

1. With grid fabric in hand, start just as you did in Unshin Exercise #1, Steps 1–3 *(page 59)*.

2. Coming from the back of the fabric, insert the needle at the intersection of 2 grid lines. **Note:** If you are using dots instead of a full grid, bring the needle up through the center of the dot. *fig. V*

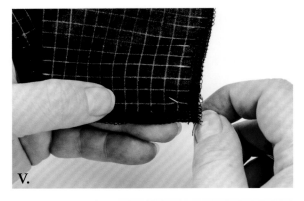

3. Collect the needle and fabric as in Unshin Exercise #1, Steps 4–8 *(pages 59–61)*. You will make the same rocking motion for the running stitches, but your stitch length will be determined by the distance between the intersections on your grid. *fig. W*

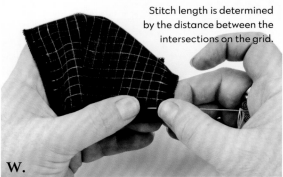

Stitch length is determined by the distance between the intersections on the grid.

4. With your needle hand, rock the needle down so the tip enters the fabric at the next unworked grid line intersection. *fig. X*

5. With your needle hand, rock the needle up so the tip comes up through the fabric at the next unworked grid line intersection. You should notice here that you are gathering more fabric onto the needle with each stitch than you did in Exercise #1. This is because the stitches here are longer and cover more fabric per stitch. *fig. Y*

6. Continue to rock the needle, repeating Steps 4 and 5 to make running stitches, until you come to the end of the row. End your row with your needle point under the fabric about ¼″ to ½″ (0.6 to 1.2 cm) from the edge of the swatch.

You will have a handful of gathered fabric and stitches in your needle hand, so it's time for the push and pull. *fig. Z*

7. Brace your needle against the palm thimble, and hold the gathered fabric near the tip of the needle in place with the thumb and middle finger of your fabric hand so it doesn't move with the needle. Make sure your grip is firm enough to hold the fabric in place but loose enough to allow the needle to slide through your fingers. With the palm thimble, push the needle as far as possible through the gathered fabric. *fig. AA*

8. Grab the gathered fabric again with your fabric hand by pinching the gathered fabric against the needle at the point where the needle tip comes out of the fabric. This will keep the gathered fabric from exploding off the tip of the needle. *fig. BB*

9. With your needle hand, pull the fabric across the length of the thread while securely holding the needle with your fabric hand. *fig. CC*

Z.

AA.

BB.

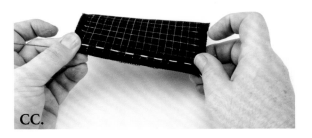

CC.

10. While still pinching the fabric and knot end of the thread with your needle hand, give the fabric at the end of the row a gentle pull with your fabric hand to give a final check for evening out the stitches. This should cause a number of the stitches to pop up on the surface of the fabric. *fig. DD*

DD.

11. Still pinching the fabric and knot end of the thread with your needle hand, gently pull on the needle end of the thread with your fabric hand until the stitches even out and lie neatly along the length of the fabric. Your goal is to have no stitches popped up above the surface of the fabric. *fig. EE*

First row complete! Happy dance then on to row 2!

EE.

12. With the top side of your fabric facing you, rotate your work 180° so your needle is again on the needle-hand side. *fig. FF*

Row 2 will consist of the same running stitches as row 1, but the stitches of row 2 will be offset from row 1.

13. Push the tip of the needle from the back to the top of the fabric at the intersection of 2 grid lines that is one space offset from where you ended your last row. *fig. GG*

FF.

GG.

14. Pull the thread through, leaving the safety loop (*page 65*). *fig. HH*

15. Repeat Steps 4–9.

16. As you did in Step 10, pinch the fabric with your needle hand, but now include the safety loop you left at the beginning of the row rather than the knot. The safety loop is now where the knot was in the previous row. *fig. II*

17. Now, still pinching the fabric and safety loop end of the thread with your needle hand, gently pull on the needle end of the thread with your fabric hand until the stitches even out and lie neatly along the length of the fabric. Your goal is to have no stitches popped up above the surface of the fabric. *fig. JJ*

HH.

II.

JJ.

Tip: The Goldilocks Loop Zone

Be sure that the loop between your rows is just right, not too tight or too loose. See Tip: The Goldilocks Loop Zone (*page 66*) in the Unshin Exercise #1 instructions for examples.

NEXT STITCHES

Congratulations! You have now successfully completed two rows of offset running stitches. Now repeat those rows a few more times to really cement your new skills in your muscle memory. Remind yourself of The Stitcher's Promise (*page 11*) and enjoy the process of learning a new skill you will be able to apply in ways you haven't even dreamed of yet.

> *Note: A Gathering of Stitches*
>
> *You are practicing here with small swatches of fabric and have gathered the fabric and stitches onto your needle for an entire row. Once you move on to larger pieces of fabric, you'll find you will need to stitch until you can't hold any more fabric securely in your fabric hand, but you aren't at the end of the row. In that case, gather the stitched fabric onto your needle until your fabric hand is comfortably full, push and pull the needle and thread, and start again. When you start your next section of stitches, be careful that you insert the needle so the length of your first starting stitch is the same as the rest of your stitches.*

OTHER USEFUL STITCHES

Half-Backstitch

For securing a row of moyouzashi running stitches.

For securing long rows of moyouzashi, we borrowed from our hand-quilting backgrounds and make one half-backstitch for every "needle length" of stitches. This locks the fabric in place and prevents it from slipping up and down the length of thread and bunching up.

1. Make your last running stitch with your needle under the fabric.

2. Bring the needle up the distance of one under-stitch and one over-stitch from the last stitch made.

3. Pull the thread all the way through the fabric. *fig. A*

4. Check that your stitches are all even and laying neatly in line with your fabric. *fig. B*

5. Insert the needle back the length of one running stitch. *fig. C*

A.

B.

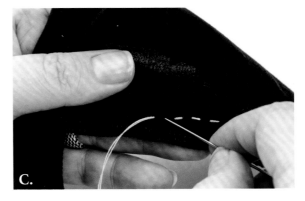
C.

6. Bring the needle up through the fabric the distance of one under-stitch beyond the last stitch on the top. *fig. D*

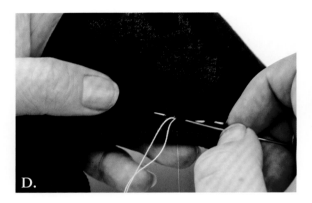

D.

7. Snug up the thread so the half-backstitch matches the neighboring stitches. *fig. E*

8. Continue with the running stitch as usual.

E.

Ladder Stitch (Slip Stitch)

For closing up the openings of bagged pieces or pillows.

This stitch goes by *ladder stitch* or *slip stitch*, depending on who taught you to do it. We use this stitch to invisibly close up the seams of bagged pieces like the throw *(page 144)* or the pillows *(page 104)*.

1. Bring the needle up from the inside of the fold in the seam allowance. This hides the knot inside the fold. *fig. F*

2. Sewing only through the folded fabric of the seam allowance, make a small stitch on the opposite side of the seam. Your needle should go into the fabric adjacent to where it just came out, behind the fold to hide the thread. The stitch should be no larger than ¼″ (6 mm) or your finished seam will pucker. *fig. G*

F.

G.

3. Make a small stitch on the opposite side of the seam. Again, your needle should go into the fabric directly across from where it just came out, traveling behind the fold no further than ¼" (6 mm). *fig. H*

4. Repeat Steps 2 and 3, pulling on your thread to close up the seam every few stitches. When you pull the thread to close the seam, be careful not to pucker the seam. *figs. I-J*

> **Note**
> *If your seam puckers, you have pulled your thread too tightly or your stitches are too large. Take the time to do it right, and don't be afraid to take out stitches until you find the thread tension and stitch size that is right for your fabric.*

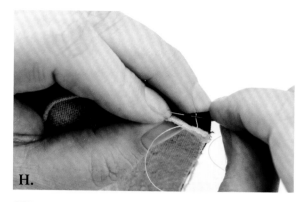
H.

I.

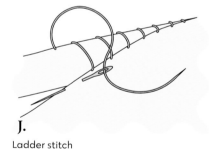
J.
Ladder stitch

READING SASHIKO PATTERN CHARTS

Sashiko charts are the pictorial representation of the pattern you are stitching. Whether it is a basic offset crosses pattern *(page 86)* or a more complex pattern, such as asanoha *(page 101)*, being able to decipher the chart correctly is the key to sashiko stitching success.

How you read the chart will depend on whether you are working hitomezashi or moyouzashi stitches. We'll break each style down for you later—but the basics are the same. When you look at a sashiko stitch chart, you are looking at the finished stitch pattern as it appears on your fabric. Although an arrow might be pointing up, down, or diagonally, the work in your hands will always be stitched horizontally: right to left for right-handed stitchers or left to right for left-handed stitchers. You will turn the work in your hands as you move along.

Note: Hey Lefties!
Reading stitch charts is the same for left-handed stitchers as it is for right-handed stitchers. The only difference is in the initial horizontal rows. The chart will tell you to work from right to left but you will work in the mirror image, left to right. The end result is the same. If you get confused, ignore the direction of this first arrow and just stitch so your pattern matches the chart.

The sashiko charts in this book generally include:

- A background grid to get you started

- Lines to indicate where over-stitches originate and terminate

- Numbers to indicate the order in which the rows of stitches are worked

- Arrows indicating the direction of work in relation to the finished stitch pattern

- Occasionally, dotted lines to indicate moving to the next row, under-stitches, or where the thread is carried under sections of fabric to connect two lines of stitches (not necessarily in rows)

Finally, there is an order to the sequence of rows in a sashiko stitch pattern. In the chart, the order of operation is generally indicated by a number next to the line. A number 1 next to the line indicates that is the first line to be worked, a number 2 indicates that is the second line to be worked, and so on. Not all stitch charts you encounter will be this well marked, but we have made sure our stitch charts have those indicators. When you encounter stitch charts without such details, you can use our charts as a general rule of thumb and determine the best order of operation.

As long as you can decipher those directions you can make any pattern in this book!

▌ READING STITCH CHARTS FOR HITOMEZASHI STITCHES

Let's take a look at a basic hitomezashi chart that you will encounter often: offset crosses. This stitch pattern is the basis for some of the most iconic patterns in the genre. Once you can "see" this stitch pattern in the first rows of more complex patterns, you can decipher most other patterns you encounter even without a chart to follow.

Offset Crosses

This chart shows the pattern is built on a 1:1 grid—the grid blocks are equal in width and height. The numeral 1 with the arrow pointing to the left indicates Step 1 is to stitch the horizontal rows with the stitch length being the width of one grid space. At the end of the first row, finish with your thread below your work, then move up and in one grid space and make a row of stitches that are offset from the previous row. Stitch all of the horizontal lines first.

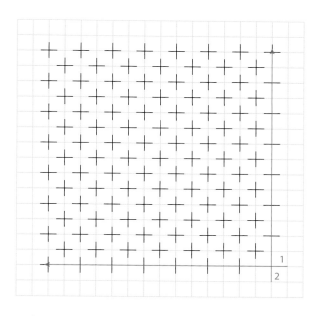

Step 2 shows an arrow pointing up, indicating these are your vertical rows. More to the point, the chart shows you to stitch offset rows directly over the stitches from Step 1. Each stitch originates and terminates in the center of a grid space, the same length as the stitches in Step 1. At the end of the first row, end with your thread below your work and move up one grid space. On your returning row, stitch in the offset spaces from the previous row. Simple enough!

The only time stitches cross in hitomezashi is when making these perpendicular crossed stitches. Any diagonal lines will leave a small space just shy of the "points" of your cross or the center of the cross. You will find that your diagonal stitches in any stitch pattern based on offset crosses will be slightly shorter than the main crossed stitches in order to fit in the grid.

Rice Stitch

Let's add another step to the horizontal and vertical lines: diagonal lines.

This stitch uses offset crosses as a base to build upon. Going back to the rules we talked about earlier, we know that we do all the horizontal lines, then the vertical lines, and then we take on the diagonals, which you can see in the chart by taking note of the numerals 3 and 4 with arrows indicating the direction of the work.

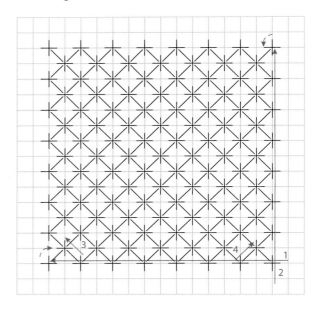

Step 3 tells you to stitch your left-leaning diagonal lines, starting in the upper left space between the arms of the cross and ending in the space between the lower right arms of the cross one row above.

Step 4 is identical to Step 3, just leaning to the right.

Note: Diagonals Do Not Cross the Crosses

Important: *Note that the diagonal lines leave a small space just shy of the center of each cross. They do not start or stop directly under the center point. As a result, your under-stitch is much smaller than the over-stitch. The only lines that cross are the vertical and horizontal. You will find that your diagonal stitches in any stitch pattern based on offset crosses will be shorter than the main crossed stitches. The difference is hardly noticeable in some patterns but remarkably so in others.*

Now for something completely different!

Rice Flower Stitch

This, too, is a hitomezashi stitch chart, but you will first notice that none of the origin or termination points for any row touches the intersection of the grid; they start and stop just short of it. Your stitches are a tad bit smaller than the grid itself. The end result of this slightly shorter stitch is that your stitches don't start or end in the same hole as any other stitch, making your final stitch pattern appear clean and even. The intersection around where the stitches point will create the optical illusion of being a dot or small circle.

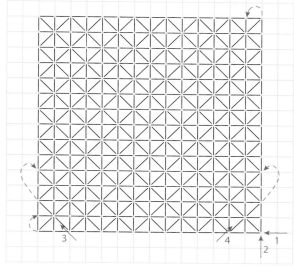

1. In this stitch chart, each row is worked the same way—work the line of stitches in every grid space with the over-stitch just shy of being as long as a grid space. The under-stitch is very small, just under the grid intersection point.

First, work the horizontal stitches. At the end of each row, move up 1 grid space to start a new row.

2. Work the vertical stitches, also with 1 grid space between rows.

3. Work the left-leaning diagonal stitches, but move 2 grid spaces between rows.

4. Stitch the right-leaning diagonal stitches, also moving 2 grid spaces between rows, so you are stitching in the diagonal spaces missed in Step 3.

Ta-da! That's all there is to it.

Persimmon Flower

One of Jason's favorite stitches is persimmon flower. This pattern is made using a series of offset running stitches with one occasional row of stacked running stitches (*page 85*) in a repeating interval. (Stacked running stitches are worked in exactly the same pattern as the previous row; offset running stitches are worked in the alternating spaces.) Each grid space has one stitch, either an over or an under, so there are no skipped spaces. It's always over one, under one, over one, under one …

To make it easier to read this chart, think about whether the first stitch is over or under the first grid space. If it over the first space, we will label it as an "O" on the chart. If it is under the first grid space, we will label it as a "U."

1. With a 1:1 grid drawn, stitch a series of horizontal offset running stitches and stacked running stitches from bottom to top in the following pattern: O, U, O, O, U, O, O, U, O, O … (the repeating pattern being U, O, O). *fig. A*

2. Stitch a series of offset running stitches and stacked running stitches from right to left in the following pattern repeat: O, U, O, O, U, O, U, U.

This is what it would look like on its own (*fig. B*):

Because you have already created the horizontal base rows, here is what the final stitch pattern will look like (*fig. C*):

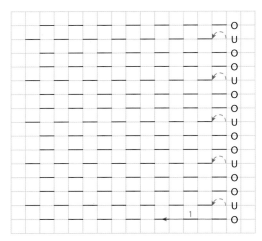

A. Persimmon flower horizontal rows

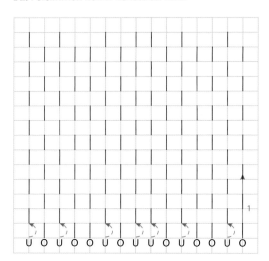

B. Persimmon flower vertical rows

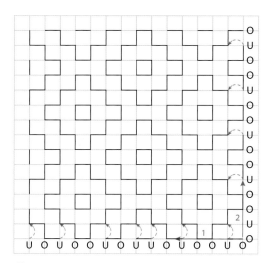

C.

Persimmon flower stitched

You will find that as you work persimmon flower and its variations, you will begin to be able to easily read your stitches. That is, you will be able to look at the stitches as they lie on the fabric and know what row to work next without referencing a chart. You will also be able to tell if a row of the pattern repeat is not correct and be able to fix it quickly. When—notice we said *when*, not *if*—you notice a row not making the pattern correctly after a few stitches, simply pull out that row and change the starting point from over to under (or under to over) to give you the correct stitch pattern.

Tip: Draw It Out

If you have problems seeing whether to start with an over- or under-stitch, draw the lines of the final pattern over the grid in a washable pen or pencil. It's not cheating! It's just keeping your sanity intact until you learn to read the stitches better, or on those days when you just don't want to think that hard.

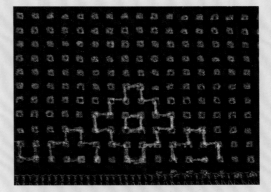

Persimmon flower drawn on a grid

STITCH PATTERNS BASED ON MOYOUZASHI STITCHES

Moyouzashi stitch patterns are slightly different from hitomezashi.

Moyouzashi sashiko charts will include:

- Occasionally, a background grid to get you started.

- Unbroken lines to indicate the lines of stitches. Origin and terminating points may not be apparent due to the nature of moyouzashi stitch patterns.

- Arrows indicating the direction of work. We no longer always rely on the horizontal, then vertical, then diagonal rule from hitomezashi. Indicators are given in the stitch chart where that rule is not used.

- Occasionally, numbers to indicate the steps.

- Occasionally, dotted lines to indicate moving to the next row or under-stitches.

Because you are no longer restricted to straight lines on a grid, there may not be any horizontal or diagonal lines in the pattern at all. For example, linked seven treasures *(below)* is comprised of interlinking circles.

Linked Seven Treasures

This pattern is stitched in a continuous line that waves in quarter-circles. You will be tempted to stitch each individual circle, but fight this urge. You will have greater success working the wavy lines moving up and down the fabric.

The chart does not tell you to watch out for areas where the lines connect or overlap. It assumes you know one of the basic rules of moyouzashi sashiko: Lines do not cross on top of the fabric.

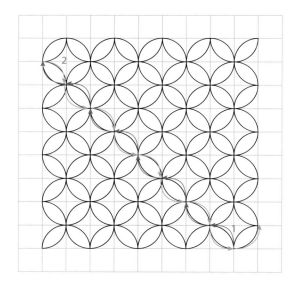

Asanoha (Hemp Leaf)

This is the one of the most beautiful and iconic patterns in the lexicon of sashiko stitches. It is also one of the most difficult patterns in this book. But don't let that stop you! Once you break down the stitch chart into its step-by-step components, you'll find the hemp leaf stitch pattern to be one of the most enjoyable and satisfying patterns to draw and stitch.

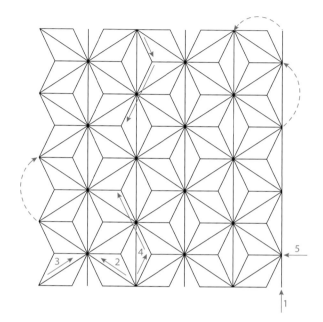

First you will notice this pattern is built on a rectangular grid, 1:1½.

1. Stitch the straight vertical rows.

2. Stitch the diagonal left-leaning rows.

3. Stitch the diagonal right-leaning rows.

4. Stitch the bending vertical rows.

5. Stitch the horizontal rows, floating the thread behind the fabric between sections.

Remember to skip the areas where the lines intersect. There are no crossed stitches on top of the work in moyouzashi. The centers of your hemp leaf pattern will look like tiny starbursts when you are done *(page 101)*.

If you break down the moyouzashi charts into sections like this, you will be able to follow any stitch chart you encounter!

SASHIKO STITCH DIRECTORY

Hitomezashi Stitches

Stitches are listed in order of difficulty with notes to make them easier to complete.

RUNNING STITCHES

Stacked Running Stitches

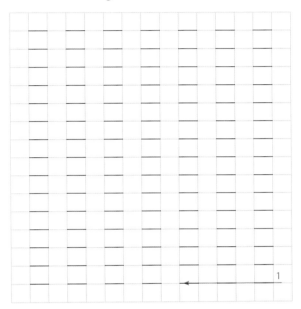

Offset Running Stitch

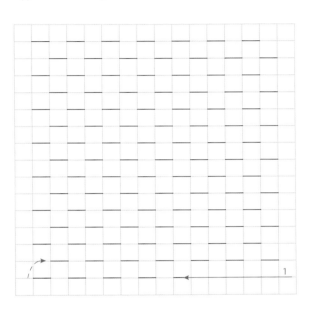

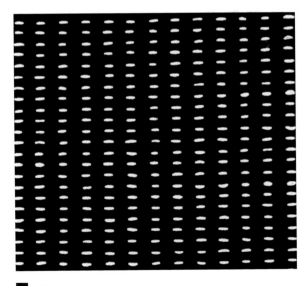

> ## Note
> *Two lines of offset running stitches worked around the edge of patches not only does a great job of securing the fabric in place but also allows the edges to fray up to the point of the running stitches but no further. The effect is a little or a lot of fab fraying, depending on how far from the edge you place your stitches.*

▍ OFFSET CROSSES AND VARIATIONS

Offset Crosses

Rice Stitch

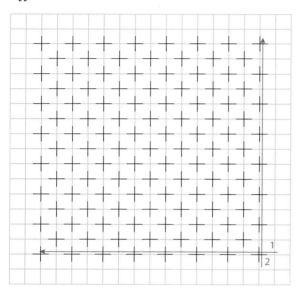

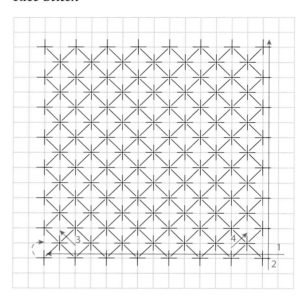

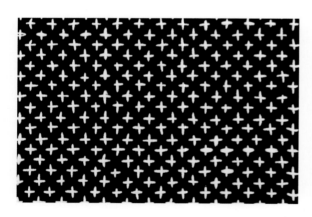

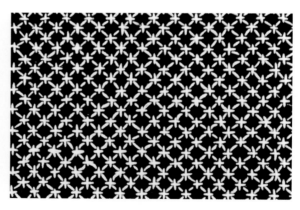

Rice Stitch Variation 1

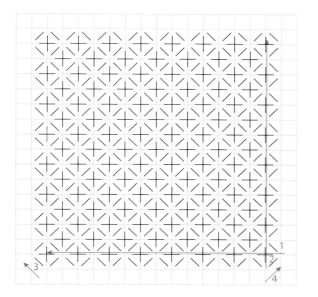

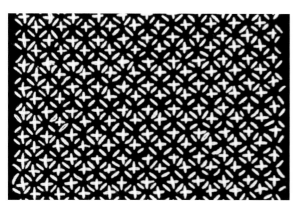

Rice Stitch Variation 2 (4-Way Cross)

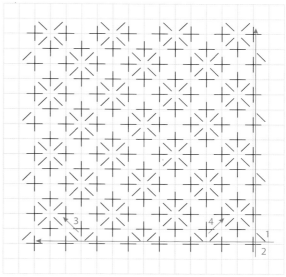

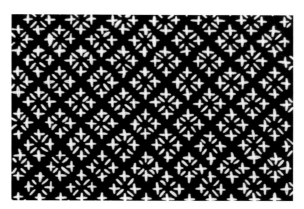

Working the diagonals in only every other row creates the illusion that the crosses were stitched in groupings of 4. We *love* this pattern!

Zigzag Crosses

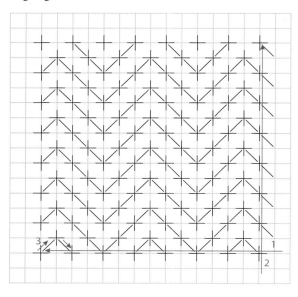

Chained Crosses

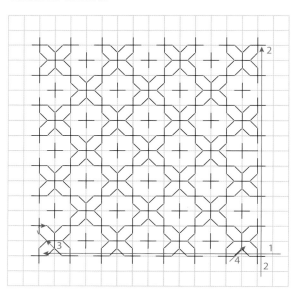

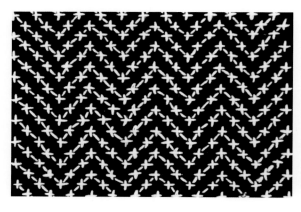

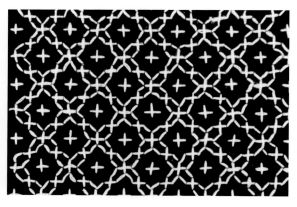

Boxes

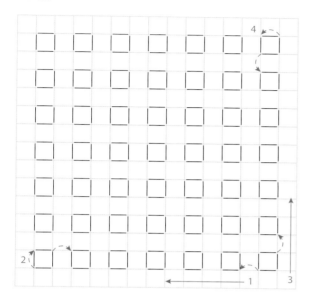

Boxes Variation 1

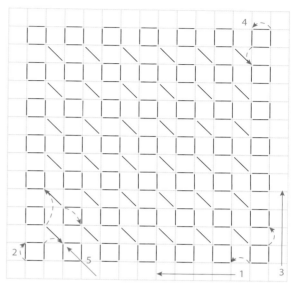

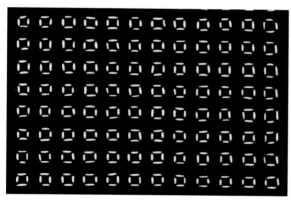

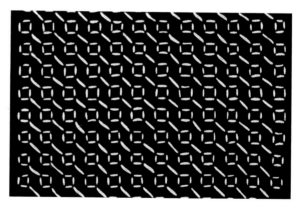

▌ PERSIMMON FLOWER AND VARIATIONS

Persimmon Flower

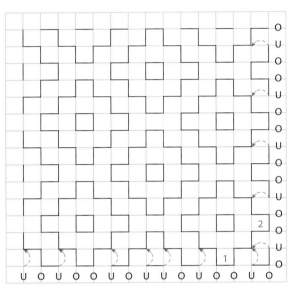

O = First stitch is over. U = First stitch is under.

Double Persimmon Flower

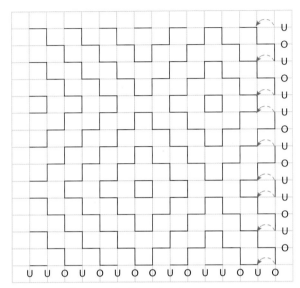

O = First stitch is over. U = First stitch is under.

Stitched like standard persimmon flower, with more offset running stitch *(page 85)* rows between each set of stacked running stitch *(page 85)* rows.

Mountain Form

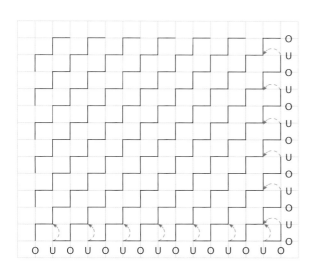

O = First stitch is over. U = First stitch is under.

All horizontal rows are stitched with rows of offset running stitches *(page 85)*. Vertical rows are also stitched with rows of offset running stitch. This will give the appearance of steps going up and down a mountain. *Bonus:* Add one set of stacked running stitches *(page 85)* anywhere in the pattern and your steps change direction! Try it for yourself.

Mountain Form Variation

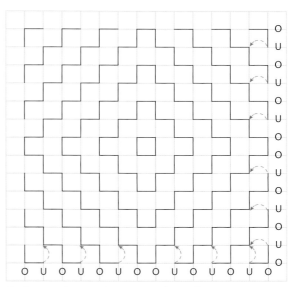

O = First stitch is over. U = First stitch is under.

The addition of one stacked running stitch row in the horizontal set up rows and one in the vertical will give the appearance of a single persimmon flower motif surrounded by increasing lines. Centering these stacked rows will give the illusion of ever-expanding growth that creates a dramatic visual effect. Try starting these on the side or corner of a boro patch to see what happens!

▌ HITOMEZASHI STITCHES WITHOUT CROSSING STITCHES

Rice Flower Stitch   *Stacked Lines*

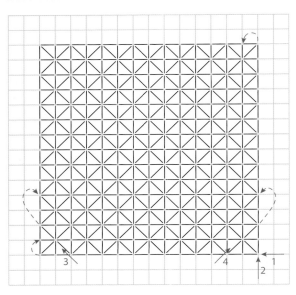   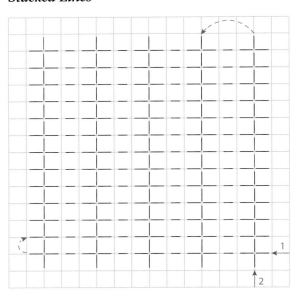

   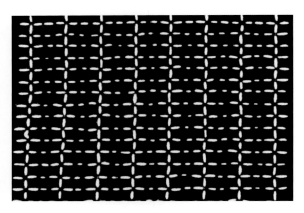

Stacked Lines Variation

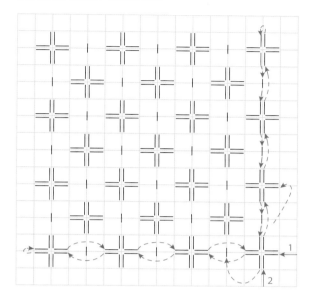

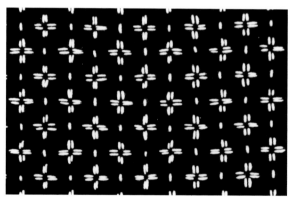

Star Stitch

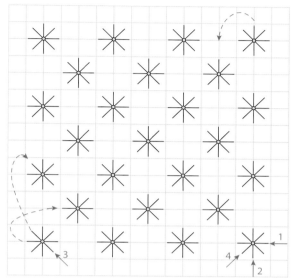

▌ WOVEN PATTERNS

These stitches are very flashy and fun to play with. Try them in different colored threads from your base stitches.

Woven Pattern 1

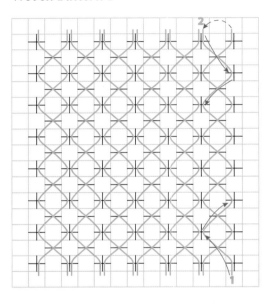

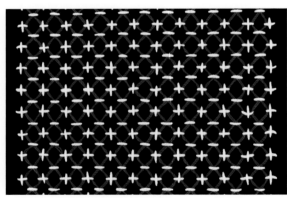

This first woven pattern is built on a base of offset crosses *(page 86)* where only every other row is crossed. The weaving is performed from the base of the first cross on the bottom right. Move from under the left-side bar of the first cross, up and under the bar diagonally above, under the right-side bar of the cross diagonally above, and then up again through the center bar to the next cross in the pattern.

Woven Pattern 2

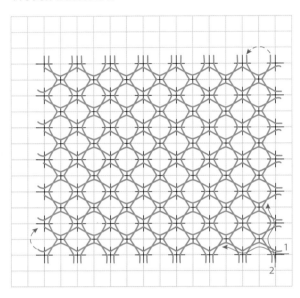

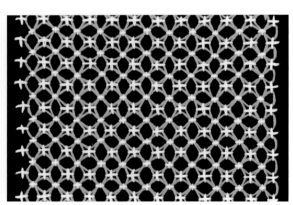

This pattern is built from a base of offset crosses where the horizontal and vertical stitch of the offset row are half the length of a normal stitch. Weave all horizontal lines first, then the vertical.

Woven Pattern 3

This pattern is built from a base of offset running stitches *(page 85)*. It is worked over 7 rows in 4 steps.

After working offset running stitches, turn your work 90° so the stitches appear vertical.

1. Weave through the bottom right-hand stitch of row 1. Skipping the stitch on row 2, move up to the second stitch 2 rows above (row 4), coming back down to the next unworked stitch in row 1. Move across the row in this fashion.

2. Follow the same pattern starting on row 3, weaving through the stitches on row 3 up to row 6, skipping the stitches on row 4 and back down to the next unworked stitch in row 3.

3. Weave from row 5 back down to the skipped stitch in row 2, then back to the second stitch in row 5.

4. Weave from row 7 back down to the first stitch in row 4, then back to the second stitch in row 7.

Begin the steps again from Step 1, with row 7 becoming the new row 1.

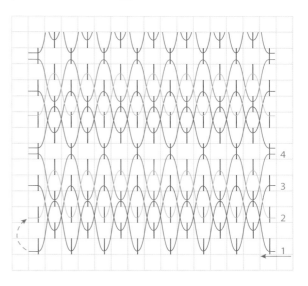

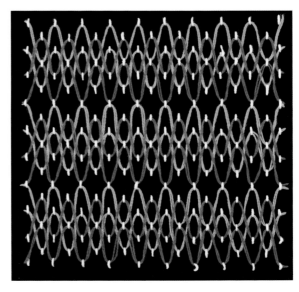

Moyouzashi Stitches

Stitches are listed in shape categories with any added notes to make them easier to stitch.

STRAIGHT-LINE PATTERNS

Spiral

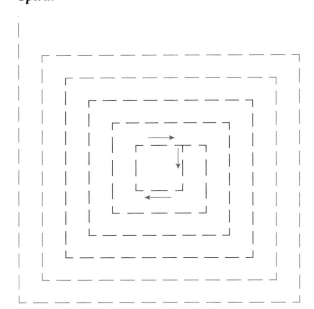

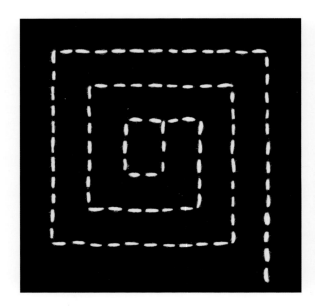

Begin in the center of the spiral and work outward.

Concentric Squares

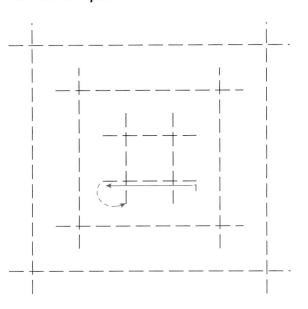

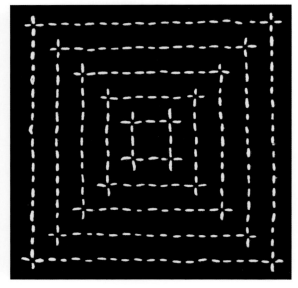

By adding more stitches to either the horizontal or vertical lines, you can easily turn this into concentric rectangles.

▍CIRCULAR PATTERNS

Linked Seven Treasures

Blue Ocean Waves

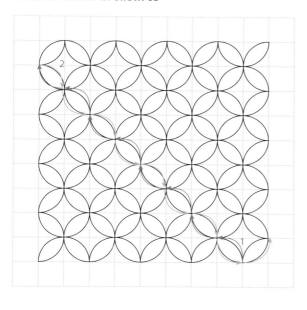

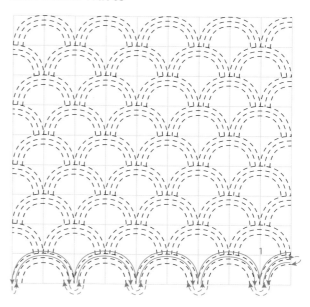

Blowing Grasses

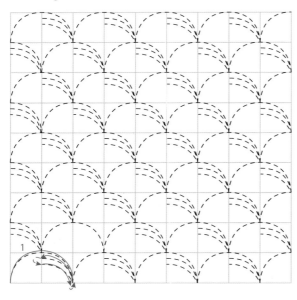

Pinwheels

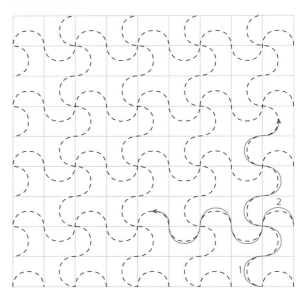

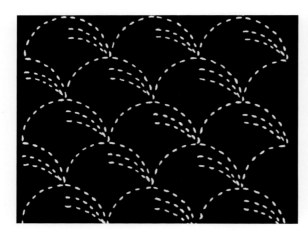

▌DIAMOND PATTERNS

Diamonds

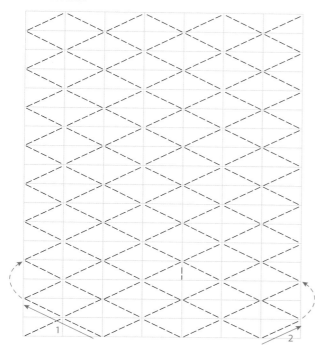

Diamonds Variation 1

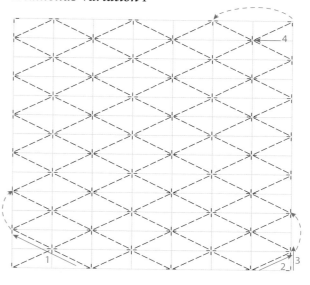

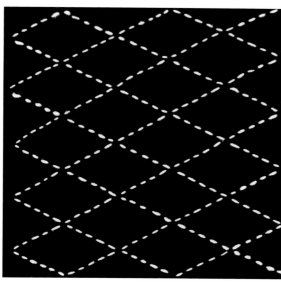

Woven Bamboo

Diamond Blue Waves

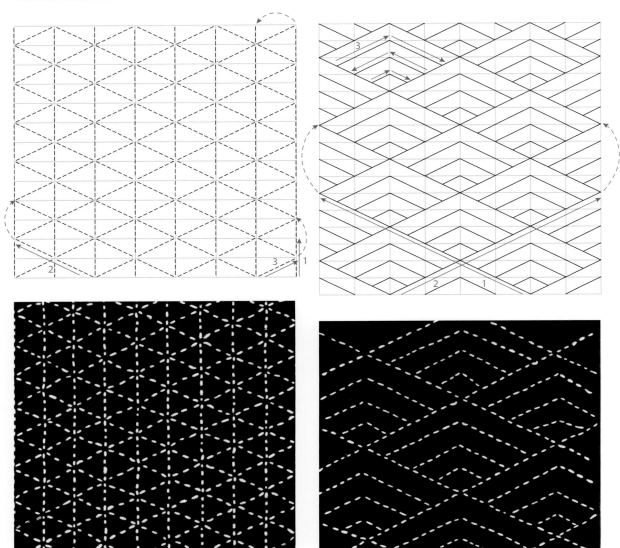

▎ASANOHA (HEMP LEAF)

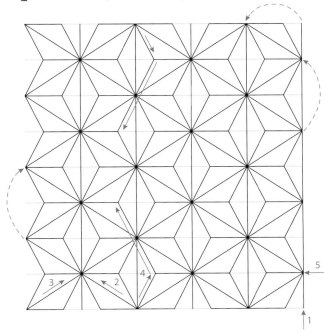

THE PROJECTS

NOTES TO THE MAKER

*Here are a few important points we would share
if we were sitting with you as you made these patterns.*

▌WHICH STITCH?

We chose the sashiko patterns in our designs
mostly for the density of the stitch patterns
and how they work in relation to our fabrics.
That said, sometimes we chose stitches simply
because we like the pattern and said, "Oh,
pretty!" when we first worked them. If you have
patterns that you reacted similarly to, feel free to
substitute them in your own pieces, keeping in
mind whether the stitches will hold the patch or
layers securely enough. As long as that criteria is
met, you are good to go!

▌LEFT AND RIGHT

Where left and right sides of a garment are
referred to in a pattern, it means left and right
sides as worn.

▌SEW/SEW

Where sewing is referenced in the instructions,
you can either machine or hand sew. Your
preference. We did a fair amount of both—other
than the sashiko stitching, which is always done
by hand.

▌DON'T BE A-FRAY-ED

Because of the nature of sashiko stitching, the
fabric is handled sometimes quite roughly. The
result can be unwanted fraying along the edges.
To prevent this, we use a zigzag or overlock stitch
or serge the edges of the fabric.

▌BE TRUE TO YOUR OWN STYLE

While we include diagrams to show you where
we placed our boro patches and sashiko stitches,
we encourage you to play a bit and use our
layouts as general guides while you experiment
with your own ideas.

With those pointers in mind … it's time to
STITCH ON!

BORO PILLOWS

Finished pillow: 16″ × 16″ (40.6 × 40.6 cm)

SMALL PANELS WITH BEAUTIFUL LITTLE TREASURES OF FABRIC AND SASHIKO make us happy, and these pillows are the perfect showcase for those panels. In the spirit of using what we have at hand to create, we used the leftover canvas from making tote bags for one pillow back and made the other from a remnant shirt from a project in conjunction with EILEEN FISHER Renew. We find projects like this to be very satisfying because they are relatively quick and mindless, and the results are not just gorgeous but make great conversation pieces.

Materials

LIGHT COTTON CANVAS OR MUSLIN:
½ yard (0.5 m) for each, front and back
(For Pillow #2 we used the front of a shirt from EILEEN FISHER Renew cut to the correct dimensions.)

RANDOM FABRICS: Enough to cover your pillow front

16″ (40.6 CM) PILLOW FORM

SASHIKO THREAD: Aurifil 12-weight cotton thread in the color(s) of your choice or other sashiko thread *(page 24)*

Cutting

LIGHT COTTON CANVAS OR MUSLIN:
Cut a square 17″ × 17″ (43.2 × 43.2 cm) for each front and back.

Tip
Zigzag or serge the edges to reduce fraying as you work.

■ Construction

Seam allowances are ½″ (1.2 cm) unless otherwise noted.

▋ BORO PATCHES

Now comes the fun part! Choose random fabrics to use as boro patches. These can be anything from scraps from old projects to new fat quarters you've been yearning to use.

▋ CHOOSING AND PLACING PATCHES

Choose larger patches and place randomly. Then add smaller patches to the sides and edges. Overlap the patches by ¼″ to ½″ (0.6 to 1.2 cm) to prevent gaps from occurring during stitching. You will not be turning under the edges of these patches. Instead you will use the nature of sashiko stitching to keep the patches in place. A certain amount of fraying is expected and wanted.

> ### Tip: Placing Patches
>
> We recommend beginning placement by laying the base fabric of the pillow right side up and randomly placing fabric scraps on it. Next, start moving the scraps around. Play with how they lie on and under each other, folding as needed to try smaller sizes.
>
> Once you settle on something you like—it may be a cluster of colors or textures together, or just a random feeling that tells you to stop—make a note of your layout. Use your phone's camera to take photos of the arrangement, making changes as needed. Keep adding patches until you are ready to stop. Once you have a layout you like, cut any folded pieces to the correct measurement, referring back to the photo on your phone (aren't cell phones handy?) to ensure you have the correct layout.

Baste the Patches

Using a washable glue stick, baste the patches to the underlying base fabric. Don't go overboard with the glue; just use enough to hold everything down as you sashiko the patches in place.

> ### Tip: Overlap
>
> Allow the patches to overlap the outside edges of the pillow's front-panel fabric by ¼″ to ½″ (0.6 to 1.2 cm) to allow for shrinkage as you stitch. Trim any overhanging edges before you sew the front panel and back panel together.

▌ SASHIKO STITCHING

1. Draw grids or trace sashiko templates over patches, being sure to cover areas of overlaps. For ideas about which sashiko patterns to use, see Sashiko Stitch Directory *(page 84)*.

2. Stitch on!

Feel free to boro both the front and back fabric or use a beautiful piece of cloth for the back. The choice is yours!

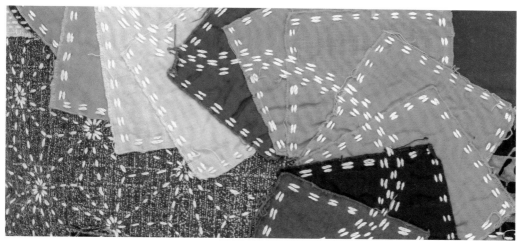

Close-up of sashiko stitching

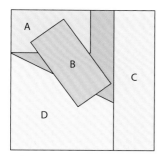

Pillow   Pillow 2

A. Stacked running stitch *(page 85)*
B. Moyouzashi lines in offset running stitch *(page 85)*
C. Star stitch *(page 93)*
D. Hemp leaf *(page 101)*
E. Offset crosses *(page 86)*
F. Persimmon flower *(page 90)*

▌ SEW THE PILLOW TOGETHER

1. Trim any overhanging patch edges from the pillow front.

2. Place the front and back squares right sides together.

3. Sew around 3 sides, using a ½″ (1.2 cm) seam allowance. Turn right side out.

4. Insert a 16″ pillow form.

5. Hand sew the remaining seam closed using the ladder stitch *(page 74)*.

REVERSIBLE KNOT BAG

Finished bag: 11½″ × 19″
(29.2 × 48.3 cm)

WE HAVE ALWAYS LOVED THE SIMPLICITY OF DESIGN and ultimate usability of these traditional Japanese knot bags. We created a reversible pattern to show off the boro patchwork we love as well as a delicious little piece of fabric we found on a flat-fold sale table. We kept the sashiko stitching simple and elegant to allow the patchwork fabric to shine.

You're going to want to make a few of these in different sizes for shopping and for carrying as a regular handbag or project bag. If you are a crocheter, knitter, or hand spinner, just put the large loop over your wrist and feed your yarn or roving out through the bag opening so you can work as you walk.

Materials

LIGHT COTTON CANVAS OR MUSLIN: ½ yard (0.5 m) for bag base fabric

COTTON OR SILK: ½ yard (0.5 m) for reversible lining

RANDOM FABRIC SCRAPS: Enough to cover the right side of your tote (See Combining Fabrics: Aesthetics and Function, *page 34,* for ideas about choosing fabric.)

SASHIKO THREAD: Aurifil 12-weight cotton thread in the color(s) of your choice or other sashiko thread *(page 24)*

Cutting

LIGHT COTTON CANVAS OR MUSLIN: Cut 1 knot-bag body.
This will be referred to as the boro fabric.

COTTON OR SILK: Cut 1 knot-bag body for the lining.

1. You don't need a pattern to cut the knot-bag body. Start with a 12½″ × 39″ (31.8 × 99.1 cm) rectangle and fold it in half to be 12½″ × 19½″ (31.8 × 49.5 cm). While it's still folded, start at the raw-edge corners and measure in 3½″ (8.9 cm); place a mark. Measure down 9¼″ (23.5 cm) from this mark and place another mark. Draw a line between each set of marks. Lay a plate or some other round template to connect the 9¼″ (23.5 cm) marks to cut the curve. It doesn't have to be exact; the unperfect nature of the cut is part of the charm.

2. While the fabric is still folded, cut the left strap handle 4″ (10.2 cm) shorter than the right.

3. Cut the lining in the same manner.

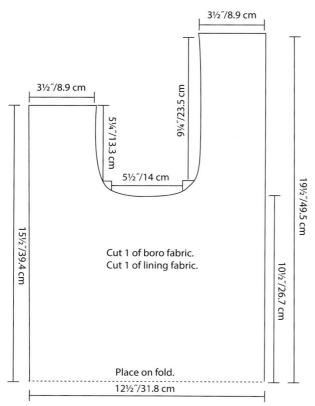

Knot-bag body cutting

Construction

Seam allowances are ½″ (1.2 cm) unless otherwise noted.

BORO PATCHES

1. Choose the fabrics for the boro patches and place as desired.

Be sure to overlap the patches by ¼″ to ½″ (0.6 to 1.2 cm) to prevent gaps from occurring during stitching.

2. Using a glue stick, baste the patches to the underlying base fabric. Don't go overboard, but use just enough to hold everything down as you stitch the patches in place. For other basting options refer to Pins, Thread, and Glue *(page 118)*.

MARK AND STITCH

1. Choose your overall sashiko theme or select individual patterns from the Sashiko Stitch Directory *(page 84)*.

2. Using an erasable marking pen, draw a base grid or trace a template over the section you want to stitch. For tips on drawing grids and templates and stitching boro patches, see Getting Ready to Stitch *(page 40)*.

3. Stitch on!

Close-up of sashiko stitching

4. With the wrong side of the boro fabric facing up, trim any overhanging fabric around the base fabric of the bag.

▌ FOLD AND SEW THE SIDES ONLY

1. Fold the boro fabric in half, right sides together.

2. Pin the sides of the bag body and the tops of the handles only. *fig. A*

3. Sew the sides and tops closed.

4. Repeat for the lining fabric.

5. Turn the boro fabric right side out

▌ STUFF THE BAGS TOGETHER

1. Insert the boro fabric into the lining fabric, right sides together.

2. Match up and pin the inside handle seams.

3. Sew the inside edges together. *fig. B*

▌ TURN OUT AND CLOSE THE OPENINGS

1. Reach into the unsewn seam and turn the bag right side out. We have a couple of unmatched or takeout chopsticks at hand to help turn out hard-to-reach spots and corners.

2. Finger-press or use an iron to press the seam allowances of the openings in both the bag and lining ¼″ (6 mm) to the inside.

3. For invisible seams, use the ladder stitch *(page 74)* to hand sew the openings closed.

After you make this and see how easy these knot bags are to make, you'll be making them for every occasion. Your friends are going to *love* them as gifts. Or you could just keep them all for yourself. You could do that.

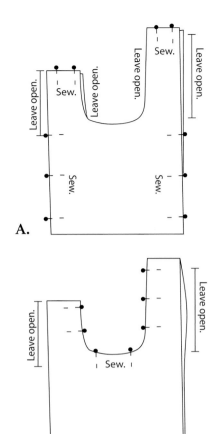

A.

B.

Use a fabric for the inside of your bag that looks *fab* when it is turned inside out.

TOO CUTE FOR THE GROCERIES TOTE

Finished tote:
14″ × 14″ (35.6 × 35.6 cm)

WHEN WE FIRST STARTED EXPERIMENTING WITH BORO AND SASHIKO, we grabbed an old tote we used for shopping. The bag was starting to fall apart, so it was a perfect candidate for boro patches and sashiko fabric reinforcing. Ever since, that tote has become a centerpiece for our trunk shows. The pockets were made from one leg of a pair of jeans and denim scraps. All the lovely little bits and pieces from projects and clothes make us happy. This project intends to delight as you build with fabrics and stitches that bring you joy.

Materials

LIGHT COTTON CANVAS OR MUSLIN: ½ yard (0.5 m) for tote body and handles

1 PAIR OF WORN DENIM JEANS, to be cut for pockets

RANDOM FABRIC SCRAPS: Enough to cover outside of your tote

SASHIKO THREAD: Aurifil 12-weight cotton thread in the color(s) of your choice or other sashiko thread *(page 24)*

Cutting

LIGHT COTTON CANVAS OR MUSLIN

- Cut 1 tote body 15″ × 30″ (38.1 × 76.2 cm).
- Cut 2 tote handles 4″ × 23″ (10.2 × 58.4 cm).

Tip: Fraying Edges

Zigzag or serge the edges to reduce fraying as you work.

DENIM JEANS

Large pockets

We're using the leg of an old pair of jeans for these 2 deep, large pockets. As you cut, keep in mind that the hem of the jeans will be the top of each large pocket. One less thing to sew!

- Lay the leg of the jeans flat with the left and right leg seams parallel. Measure and mark a rectangle 6½″ × 12″ (16.5 × 30.5 cm) centered between the side seams and including the hem. Cut along the lines of the rectangle through both layers. 2 pockets! Ta-da!

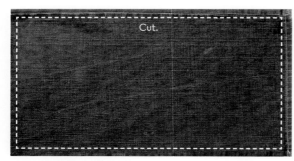

Cutting large pockets

Double pocket

- Lay the jeans with the back pockets facing up. Measure and mark a rectangle 8½″ × 7¾″ (21.6 × 19.7 cm) around one of the back pockets. Be careful to keep the sewn pocket centered in the rectangle. Cut along the lines of the rectangle.

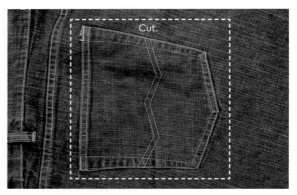

Cut a double pocket.

Tip: Easy Cutting

Since you don't want to cut through both layers this time, place a quilting ruler or large piece of plexiglass inside the jeans and under the rectangle for easy cutting around the pocket.

Construction

Seam allowances are ½" (1.2 cm) unless otherwise noted.

POCKETS

1. Lay the tote wrong side down.

2. Measure 3" (7.6 cm) down from each short edge of the tote and draw a straight line across.

3. Place the top of the first large pocket on one end of the tote along the drawn line, centered on the body of the tote as shown in the right side pockets diagram. Pin into place.

4. Place the double pocket on the opposite end of the tote, again placing the top of the pocket centered and on the drawn line. Pin into place.

5. Turn the tote facedown.

6. On the wrong side of the base fabric, place the second large pocket, matching the placement of the large pocket from Step 3, which is on the front of the tote. Pin into place.

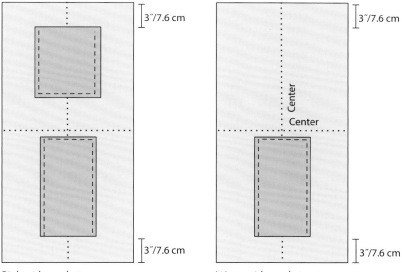

Right side pockets   Wrong side pockets

7. Machine stitch a ¼" (6 mm) seam along the right, bottom, and left edges of each pocket. When sewing the large pockets, sew through both layers at the same time.

> ### Note: No Turning Under
> *When you sew the pockets, leave the edges raw.*
> *Just place the pockets, square them up, pin, and sew.*

▌ BORO PATCHES

1. Choose the fabrics for the boro patches and place accordingly:

First, choose larger patches and place randomly; then add smaller patches to the sides and edges. Remember to overlap the patches by ¼″ to ½″ (0.6 to 1.2 cm) to prevent gaps from occurring during stitching.

Allow the patches to overlap the outside edges of the tote's base fabric by ¼″ to ½″ (0.6 to 1.2 cm) to allow for shrinkage as you stitch. Trim any overhanging edges before you sew the tote together.

▌ *Note: Mind the Gap*
Don't stress out if you do find a gap. You can always add another patch later.

2. Using a glue stick, baste the patches to the underlying base fabric. Don't go overboard, but use just enough to hold everything down as you stitch the patches in place.

- -

PINS, THREAD, AND GLUE

Remember, you have choices when it comes to basting.

• Pins are great when working with a few patches that are larger and set apart.

• Thread basting works on projects with a few more patches that overlap.

• In the case of a bag like this with *a lot* of patches overlapping in various directions, a glue stick is your friend. Basting with a glue stick allows you to make fast changes and re-center or replace at your artistic whim.

• We don't recommend using spray adhesives for boro. That gets ugly.

- -

▌MARK AND STITCH

1. Choose your overall sashiko theme or select individual patterns from the Sashiko Stitch Directory *(page 84)*.

2. Using a fabric pen or washable pen or pencil, lay out and draw a base grid or trace a template over the section to stitch down.

3. Stitch. For tips on drawing grids and templates, see Getting Ready to Stitch *(page 40)*.

Tip: Patches over Pockets

When stitching boro patches over the large and double pockets, remember to slip your hand inside the pocket to keep from sewing it closed ... not that we've ever made that mistake!

▌HANDLES

Construct the Handles

1. With the wrong side facing up, fold a ¼″ (6 mm) seam allowance along both long sides of the handles and press. *fig. A*

2. Fold in half lengthwise; pin as needed and press. *fig. B*

3. Using a sewing machine, close the long side of the handles by topstitching ⅛″ (3 mm) from the edge.

4. Sew a second line of topstitching along the folded edge ⅛″ (3 mm) from the edge to match the first. *fig. C*

Sashiko the Handles

Use offset running stitches *(page 85)* along the length of both handles to reinforce.

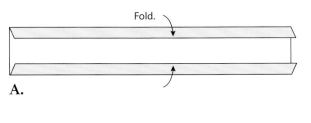

A.

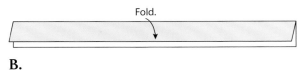

B.

C. Construct the tote handles.

▌ASSEMBLE THE TOTE

Once you are satisfied that all patches are sufficiently (and aesthetically) stitched down and your handles are reinforced, it's time to sew up the tote.

▌*Note:* **Never Really Finished**
Projects like this are never really "finished." You can always add more stitches or patches as the mood strikes you. That mood strikes us a lot.

1. Trim any overhanging edges to square up the sides of the tote.

2. With the wrong side facing up, fold down 1″ (2.5 cm) along the top of the short edge. Pin into place.

3. Sew ¼″ (6 mm) seam along the raw edge of the fold.

4. Measure in 3½″ (8.9 cm) from both the right and left edges on the *wrong side* of the tote and make a mark on the fold for each side.

5. Place the base of the handles along the sewn seam, centering on the mark. The handle should stick out above the bag body ... because that's how handles work. Pin into place. *fig. D*

6. Using a sewing machine, sew the bases of the handle into place using a box X stitch as shown in diagram.

7. Repeat Steps 2–6 for the second handle.

3½″/8.9cm   3½″/8.9cm

3½″/8.9cm   3½″/8.9cm

D. Sewing on the handles

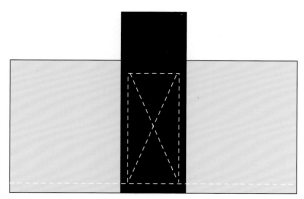

Close-up of handle box X stitch

Sew the Side Seams

1. With right sides together, sew a ½″ (1.2 cm) seam on both the left and right edges of the tote.

2. Turn right side out.

Off to the store to show off your handiwork!

Don't stop now! Customize your totes to be smaller or larger by adjusting the size of the base fabric. You can even customize those free totes you pick up at markets and events by adding patches, pockets, and stitches to your heart's content.

BORO TOOL KIT ROLL

Finished tool kit roll: 13″ × 14″ (33 × 35.6 cm) when completely open

AN ESSENTIAL FOR ANY MAKER, a tool roll keeps our most used tools and notions close at hand whether we are working in different rooms outside our studio or traveling to shows to teach. We dove into our scrap bags again for this tool roll and used parts from a pair of jeans for a project that is almost completely recycled materials.

Materials

For this project we repurposed a pair of well-worn jeans from our closet. Feel free to substitute any sturdy fabric you wish.

PAIR OF JEANS:

- 1 leg at least 15″ (38.1 cm) deep when cut open at a side seam, or substitute ½ yard (0.5 m) denim or other sturdy fabric, for roll-kit outside

- 2 repurposed belt loops or 2 strips ½″ × 3½″ (1.2 × 8.9 cm) for spool straps

- 1 denim patch 8″ × 4″ (20.3 × 10.2 cm) for tool pocket (We used the top of a jeans pocket.)

- 1 denim patch or felt 6″ × 4″ (15.2 × 10.2 cm) for needle keeper

- 1 denim strip 1″ × 16″ (2.5 × 40.6 cm) for tie

SOLID QUILTING COTTON: 1 fat quarter or 2 fat eighths for inside body and inside flap

ASSORTED FABRIC SCRAPS for boro patches on outside body (We used a floral and 3 solids.)

SASHIKO THREAD: Aurifil 12-weight cotton thread in the color(s) of your choice or other sashiko thread *(page 24)*

DOUBLE-SIDED FUSIBLE LIGHT INTERFACING (such as fast2fuse LIGHT Interfacing by C&T Publishing): ⅓ yard (0.3 m)

LEATHER OR ELASTIC: 2 pieces 14″ (35.6 cm) in length for thread loops

SEW-ON SNAP: 1 snap, size 4

Cutting

JEANS OR DENIM

- Cut the outer backing:

1. Open one seam on the leg of the jeans and lay flat, wrong side up, so the second seam is running crosswise in the center of the fabric.

2. Square off the fabric as needed by cutting off the hem.

3. Measure 6″ (15.2 cm) up from the top edge of the remaining seam (in the middle of the fabric) and make a mark 16″ (40.6 cm) long.

4. Measure 9″ (22.9 cm) down from the bottom edge of the same seam and make a mark 16″ (40.6 cm) long. You should have a rectangle 16″ × 15″ (40.6 × 38.1 cm).

- Cut 2 belt loops from a pair of jeans, or cut 2 strips ½″ × 3½″ (1.2 × 8.9 cm) for the spool straps.

- Cut 1 patch 8″ wide × 3″ high (20.3 × 7.6 cm) at one end and 4″ (10.2 cm) high at the other end for the tool pocket. We used the top of a pocket. You can also cut a rectangle 8″ × 4″ (20.3 × 10.2 cm), then trim the bottom diagonally to be 3″ (7.6 cm) at one end.

- Cut 1 rectangle 4″ × 6″ (10.2 × 15.2 cm) for the needle keeper (or substitute felt).

SOLID QUILTING COTTON

- Cut 1 rectangle 8″ × 14″ (20.3 × 35.6 cm) for the inside body.

- Cut 1 rectangle 5″ × 14″ (12.7 × 35.6 cm) for the inside flap.

ASSORTED FABRIC SCRAPS

- Cut 1 rectangle 5″ × 7″ (12.7 × 17.8 cm).

- Cut 1 rectangle 4″ × 6″ (10.2 × 15.2 cm).

- Cut 12 squares 2″ × 2″ (5.1 × 5.1 cm).

INTERFACING

- Cut 1 rectangle 8″ × 14″ (20.3 × 35.6 cm) for the inside body.

- Cut 1 rectangle 5″ × 14″ (12.7 × 35.6 cm) for the inside flap.

Boro Tool Kit Roll, all rolled up and ready to tuck into another bag!

■ Construction

Seam allowances are ½″ (1.2 cm) unless otherwise noted.

▌ BORO PATCHES

1. Choose fabrics for the boro patches and place as desired. See the diagram for how we arranged our patches.

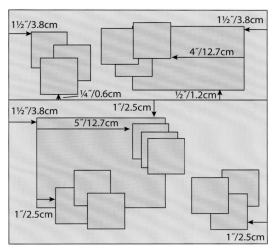

Boro patch placement

2. Using a glue stick, baste the patches to the outside body. Don't go overboard, just use enough to hold everything down as you stitch.

3. Choose your overall sashiko theme or select individual patterns from the Sashiko Stitch Directory *(page 84)*. We stitched the sample in offset running stitch *(page 85)* at 30°, with a second set of offset running stitch placed at 90° from that line.

4. Using a disappearing marking pen, draw a base grid or trace a template over the section you want to stitch. For tips on drawing grids and templates, see Getting Ready to Stitch *(page 40)*.

5. Stitch on!

Close-up of sashiko stitching

Boro Tool Kit Roll, showing the stitching on the flap

▍ MAKE THE INSIDE ROLL

1. Following the manufacturer's instructions, fuse the interfacing to the wrong side of the inside body.

2. Place the angled tool-pocket rectangle on the tool kit body, with the left and lower edges 1″ (2.5 cm) inside the edges of the tool kit body. Topstitch the left, bottom, and right edges.

> ### Tip: Overlock Edges
> For cleaner edges, serge or use an overlock stitch on your machine to sew around the raw denim edges before you install the pocket.

3. Sew vertical lines, backstitching at both ends, to make the pocket segments. We divided ours into a 1½″ (3.8 cm)-wide pocket, 4 pockets 1″ (2.5 cm) wide, and a 2½″ (6.4 cm)-wide pocket.

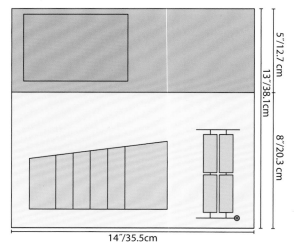

Inside roll

▍ CREATE THE THREAD HOLDER

1. Fold each piece of leather or elastic in half, creating a loop, and place them on the inside body fabric.

2. If you cut strips for the spool straps instead of using belt loops, turn under ½″ (1.2 cm) at each end of both straps.

3. Place the first spool strap over the loose ends of the leather strips.

4. Sew around all 4 sides of the strap, being sure to stitch through the leather strips.

5. Place the second spool strap as shown in the inside roll diagram *(at left)*.

6. Sew down the left side of this strap only.

7. Measure and position the bottom half of a sew-on snap to the inside roll, just under the opposite end of the spool strap.

8. Sew the top half of the snap to the wrong side of the second spool strap so it matches up with the other half of the snap.

MAKE THE INSIDE FLAP

1. Following the manufacturer's instructions, fuse the interfacing to the wrong side of the inside flap.

2. Place the needle keeper 1″ (2.5 cm) inside the left edge, matching the tip edge of the tool kit flap. Topstitch the top edge only.

ATTACH THE BACKINGS

1. Wrong sides together, place the inside body on top of the boro outside body.

2. Position the top edge snug under the seam of the jeans, leaving a 1″ (2.5 cm) seam allowance on the left, bottom, and right sides.

3. Press, attaching the back of the fusible interfacing to the wrong side of the outside body. At the same time, press the jeans seam down over the edge of the backing.

4. Repeat Steps 2 and 3 with the inside flap, positioning the bottom edge of the inside flap snug against the top side of the seam of the jeans.

FINISH THE ROLL

1. Around the entire outside body, fold a ½″ (1.2 cm) seam allowance to the inside; then fold another ½″ (1.2 cm) to just cover the edge of the inside body and flap. Pin as needed. Turn the fabric over.

2. Lay the center of the denim tie in the center of the right side of the outside body and pin in place. Turn over again.

3. Using a denim needle in your sewing machine, topstitch the folded seam as close to the edge as possible; an edge-stitch foot is handy here.

Take care when you get to the denim tie; that's a lot of fabric to sew through.

4. Topstitch around the edge again, this time ¼″ (6 mm) from the folded seam.

STORE YOUR SEWING ITEMS

1. Place pens, pencils, Hera Markers, and snips in the tool-pocket sections.

2. Store extra sashiko needles in the flap. Make sure the pointy ends stay to the back side!

3. Thread bobbins or small spools of sashiko thread through the leather strips and thread the bottom denim strip through the loops, anchoring with the snap.

4. Place the flap over the top of the tools to keep them all secure, then roll it up and tie.

Just a thought … this roll kit will look *fab* inside your Too Cute for the Groceries Tote *(page 114)* or Reversible Knot Bag *(page 108)*!

SASHIKO SAMPLER WALLHANGING

Finished wallhanging: 30˝ × 48˝ (76.2 × 121.9 cm)

THIS WALLHANGING IS A SHOWCASE FOR SOME OF OUR FAVORITE STITCHES. We grouped them together to show how different sashiko patterns build off one another to create more complex overall patterns. We love how one little change can create a showstopping effect for even the beginning stitcher. This is another piece we designed to give you creative leeway to develop and include your own boro patching and sashiko style and personality.

Note that the pattern says to turn the edges of all the patches. This is only a suggestion. Leaving ¼″ to ½″ (0.6 to 1.2 cm) of the edges free to fray will give your artwork a softer appearance.

Materials

BLUE COTTON OR MUSLIN: 1½ yards (1.4 m) for front panel

TAN COTTON OR MUSLIN: 1½ yards (1.4 m) for back panel (We used Cherrywood Hand Dyed Fabrics Cotton for the front and back panels because of its density, rich color, and ease of cutting.)

GREEN: ½ yard (0.5 m) for patch 1

EGGPLANT: ⅜ yard (0.3 m) for patch 2

SASHIKO THREAD: Aurifil 12-weight cotton thread in the color(s) of your choice *(page 24)*

Cutting

BLUE

- Cut a rectangle 31″ × 49″ (78.7 × 124.5 cm) for the front panel.

- Cut 1 oval for patch 3 (patch C). See the Sashiko Sampler Wallhanging oval pattern *(page 133)*. Photocopy or trace the pattern and lay the template on the wrong side of the fabric. Add an additional ½″ (1.2 cm) seam allowance, mark, and cut.

TAN

- Cut a rectangle 31″ × 49″ (78.7 × 124.5 cm) for the back panel.

- Cut a rectangle 9″ × 29″ (22.9 × 73.7 cm) for the rod pocket.

GREEN: Cut a rectangle 13″ × 42″ (33 × 106.7 cm) for patch 1.

EGGPLANT: Cut a rectangle 10″ × 23″ (25.4 × 58.4 cm) for patch 2.

> ### Note: Turn Under the Edges
> *Turn the edges of the rectangle patches ½″ (1.2 cm) to the wrong side and press.*

Construction

Seam allowances are ½″ (1.2 cm) unless otherwise noted.

▍WALLHANGING ASSEMBLY

1. Right sides facing, pin the front and back panels together.

2. Sew around both long sides, the top, and half of the bottom edge.

3. Clip the corners about ⅛″ (3 mm) from the sewn line. This helps the corners come out sharp when you turn the wallhanging.

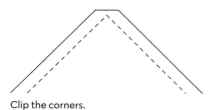

Clip the corners.

4. Turn the wallhanging right side out through the opening on the bottom.

5. Finger-press the seams flat to make sure the sides are straight and the corners are sharp.

> ### Tip: Use That Yardstick
> Insert a yardstick into the center of the throw. Push it into the corners and run it along the edges to ensure all seams are fully turned and straight. If you don't have a yardstick, a small-diameter dowel will do.

6. Quickly press to set all the seams.

7. Use the ladder stitch *(page 74)* to close the opening.

▋ BORO PATCHWORK

1. Lay the front right side up and place patches 1, 2, and 3 as shown in the placement diagram *(below)*.

2. Baste the patches to the wallhanging and sew into place using monofilament or a neutral-color thread. We recommend Aurifil Monofilament (1000 mt) or Aurifil 50 weight (color #6711).

> ### ▋ Note: Edging Options
> *For a more modern, clean-edge appearance, we used monofilament and a blind hem stitch on our BERNINA B 790 PLUS to sew the patches in place. If you want a more traditional appearance, feel free to sew the edges down using offset running stitches.*

3. Lay the wallhanging flat and hand baste the front to the back in preparation for stitching. Depending on the patches, our basting lines were about 2″ (5 cm) apart. The idea is to keep the layers of fabric from moving around while you stitch.

▋ SASHIKO STITCHING

Do all of the sashiko stitching through the patches and the front and back of the wallhanging.

1. Draw templates or grids on patches 1, 2 and 3.

2. Use the oval template to trace the shape of the 2 layered ovals at the right side of the boro oval patch.

3. Stitch sampler motifs on the patches, going through all layers.

4. Stitch diagonal lines on large areas of the front fabric to further secure the layers.

A. Woven pattern 3 *(page 95)*
B. Blowing grasses *(page 98)*
C. Linked seven treasures *(page 97)*
D. Waves 2″, ½″, ⅛″ *(page 97)*
E. Offset crosses *(page 86)*
F. Rice stitch variation 1 *(page 87)*
G. Rice stitch variation 2 *(page 87)*
H. Chained crosses *(page 88)*
I. Rice stitch *(page 86)*
J. Zigzag crosses *(page 88)*

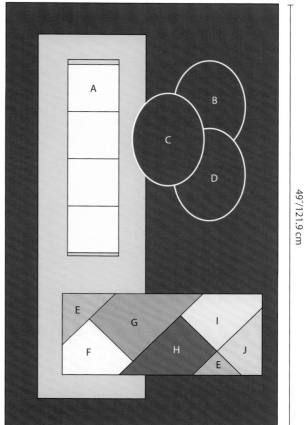

Boro and sashiko placement

▌ MAKE THE ROD POCKET

1. Fold the short edges under ¼″ (6 mm), then another ¼″ (6 mm), and press.

2. Topstitch the folded edge.

3. Fold the rod pocket in half, right sides together widthwise, and sew a ½″ (1.2 cm) seam along the long edge.

4. Turn the rod pocket right side out and press flat with the seam centered on what will be the back of the rod pocket.

5. With the rod pocket oriented horizontally, pull the top layer of fabric down, moving the top fold line ½″ (1.2 cm) toward the center. Press a new fold line. This will create a bubble of fabric that will allow the hanging rod to be inserted without distorting the front of the throw.

6. Measure 1″ (2.5 cm) down from the top of the wallhanging and hand sew both the top and bottom edges of the rod pocket into place.

Rod pocket placement

When the stitching is complete, press and display with pride.

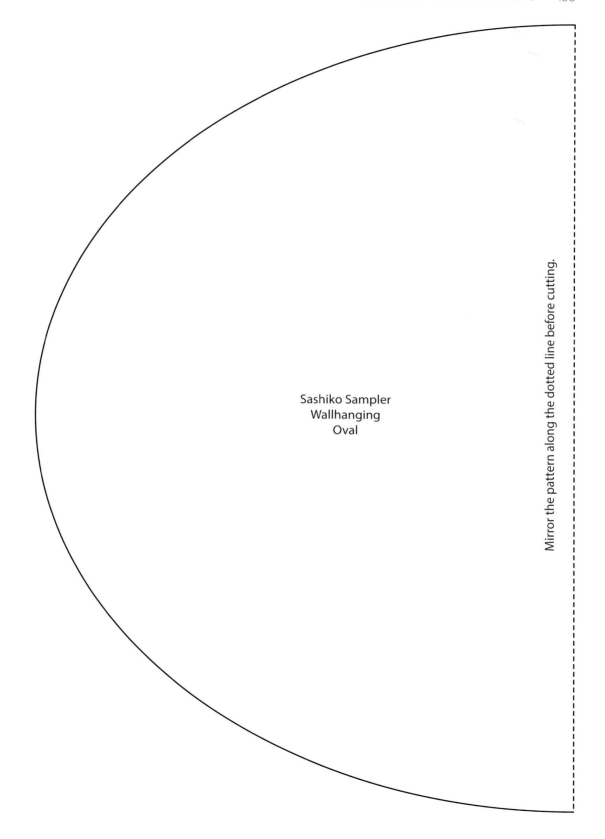

Sashiko Sampler
Wallhanging
Oval

Mirror the pattern along the dotted line before cutting.

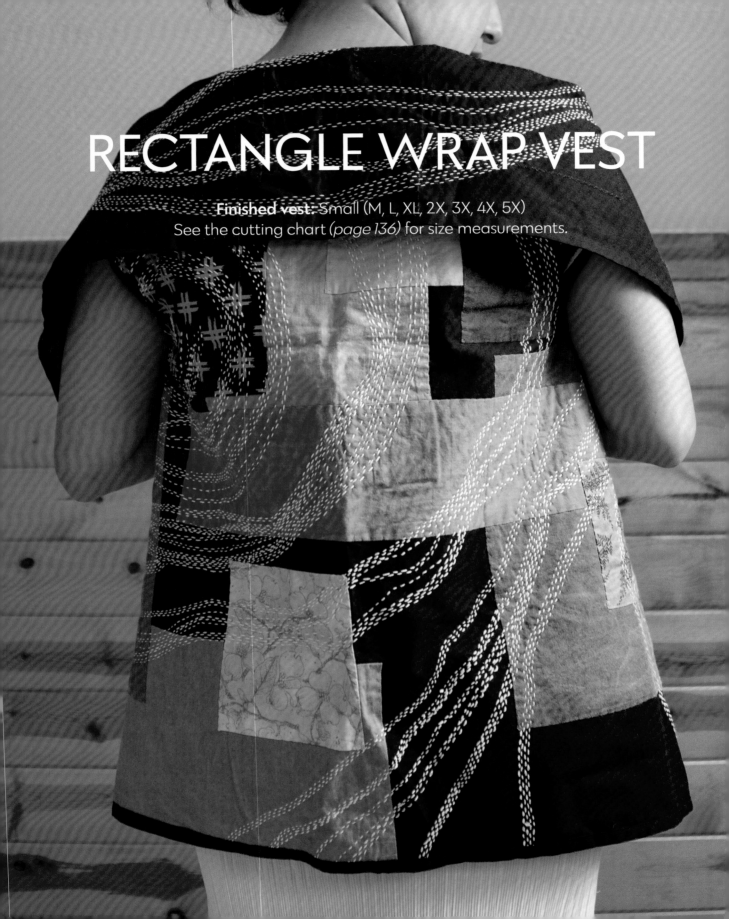

RECTANGLE WRAP VEST

Finished vest: Small (M, L, XL, 2X, 3X, 4X, 5X)

See the cutting chart *(page 136)* for size measurements.

WE LIKE USING SIMPLE SHAPES to create garments that are easy to make and easy to wear on a variety of body shapes. Here, we combined one of our favorite pieces of Japanese art with our own doodle and the abstract sashiko wave pattern to create a reversible piece of wearable art. The rectangular shape of this wrap vest allows both first-time and more experienced makers to create a wearable piece of art that shows their own personality.

For our wrap vest, we used layers of boro patchwork finished with abstract moyouzashi-style stitches worked as an abstract representation of a large wave. Our inspiration for the wave came from the iconic color woodblock print by Japanese artist Katsushika Hokusai called *Under the Wave off Kanagawa*. Growing up, Shannon used to doodle endlessly, and the wave form we use in this design is one the motifs that still remains in his doodle repertoire to this day. Feel free to follow our inspiration for your first project or let your imagination free to create your own work of art.

Materials

LIGHT COTTON CANVAS OR MUSLIN: 1⅛ (1¼, 1⅜, 1½, 1⅝, 1¾, 1⅞, 2) yards / 1 (1.1, 1.3, 1.4, 1.5, 1.6, 1.7, 1.8) m

RANDOM FABRIC SCRAPS: Enough to cover outside of your vest

SASHIKO THREAD: Aurifil 12-weight cotton thread in the color(s) of your choice or other sashiko thread *(page 24)*

SEWING THREAD: Aurifil Monofilament (1000 mt)

- -

PATTERN NOTES

This jacket is not lined. To keep the edges from fraying, we recommend serging the body piece using a 3-needle overlock or zigzag stitch along the edge.

- -

Cutting

LIGHT COTTON CANVAS OR MUSLIN

- Cut a rectangle for the vest body according to the sizes in the cutting chart *(below)*.

- Cut 2 rectangles 1¼" (3.2 cm) × the length of your armhole plus 1" (2.5 cm) for the armhole facing.

	S	M	L	XL
Shoulder-to-shoulder measurement *(Use to find your size.)*	17" (43.2 cm)	18½" (47 cm)	21½" (54.6 cm)	24" (61 cm)
Width × height of rectangle	38½" × 34½" (97.8 × 87.6 cm)	42½" × 34½" (108 × 87.6 cm)	46½" × 36½ (118.1 × 92.7 cm)	50½" × 36½" (128.3 × 92.7 cm)
Armhole depth *(Don't cut yet; just mark!)*	8" (20.3 cm)	8½" (21.6 cm)	9" (22.9 cm)	9½" (24.1 cm)
Distance between armhole opening and sides of vest	10¾" (27.3 cm)	12" (30.5 cm)	12½" (31.8 cm)	13¼" (33.7 cm)

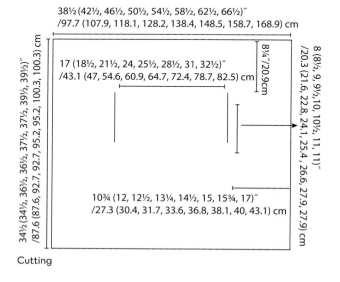

38½ (42½, 46½, 50½, 54½, 58½, 62½, 66½)" /97.7 (107.9, 118.1, 128.2, 138.4, 148.5, 158.7, 168.9) cm

34½ (34½, 36½, 36½, 37½, 37½, 39½, 39½)" /87.6 (87.6, 92.7, 92.7, 95.2, 95.2, 100.3, 100.3) cm

17 (18½, 21½, 24, 25½, 28½, 31, 32½)" /43.1 (47, 54.6, 60.9, 64.7, 72.4, 78.7, 82.5) cm

8¼"/20.9cm

8 (8½, 9, 9½, 10, 10½, 11, 11)" /20.3 (21.6, 22.8, 24.1, 25.4, 26.6, 27.9, 27.9) cm

10¾ (12, 12½, 13¼, 14½, 15, 15¾, 17)" /27.3 (30.4, 31.7, 33.6, 36.8, 38.1, 40, 43.1) cm

Cutting

Note: Armholes

Mark the armhole openings after you cut out the rectangle, placing them 8¼" (21 cm) from the top of the garment. See the cutting chart for the distance between the armhole openings and the sides of the vest. However, do not cut the armhole openings early. You will cut the armholes when you create the facing, after the boro and sashiko work is complete.

RANDOM FABRIC SCRAPS: Cut boro patches. We included ¼" (6 mm) seam allowances to be turned under, but if you decide to use raw-edge patches, omit the seam allowance.

	2X	3X	4X	5X
Shoulder-to-shoulder measurement *(Use to find your size.)*	25½" (64.8 cm)	28½" (72.4 cm)	31½" (80 cm)	32½" (82.6 cm)
Width × height of rectangle	54½" × 37½" (138.4 × 95.3 cm)	58½" × 37½" (148.6 × 95.3 cm)	62½" × 39½" (158.8 × 100.3 cm)	66½" × 39½" (168.9 × 100.3 cm)
Armhole depth *(Don't cut yet; just mark!)*	10" (25.4 cm)	10½" (26.7 cm)	11" (27.9 cm)	11" (27.9 cm)
Distance between armhole opening and sides of vest	14½" (36.8 cm)	15" (38.1 cm)	15¾" (40 cm)	17" (43.2 cm)

▌ Construction

Seam allowances are ½" (1.2 cm) unless otherwise noted.

▌ BORO PATCHES

You have two options here. Place individual patches with no turned edges all over the right side of the vest, making a collage of fabric like we did in with the Too Cute for the Groceries Tote *(page 114)*, or use fewer, larger patches with turned edges like we did with the Lotus Pond Throw *(page 144)*.

1. Choose the fabrics for the boro patches by laying them on the vest fabric. Play with the layout, noting the ¼" (6 mm) seam allowance if you are turning under the edges of the large patches. Leave at least 1" (2.5 cm) around the border of the vest free of patches. This will be turned under at the last step.

Tip: Placing Patches

Lay a few fat quarters or large scraps on the vest. Fold these into patch sizes you like and make note of the arrangement. First, choose larger patches and place randomly; then add smaller patches to the sides and edges. Use your phone's camera to take photos of the arrangement, making changes as needed. This lets you see the overall image. Once you have a layout you like, cut any folded pieces to the correct measurement, referring back to the photo on your phone to ensure you have the correct layout.

The following diagram shows the placement of the patches for our sample.

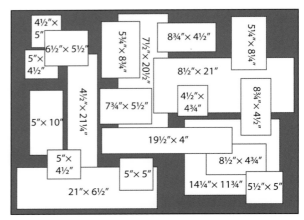

Boro patch placement

2. Turn the edges under ¼″ (6 mm) and press.

3. Pin the boro patches in place on the vest.

4. Machine sew the patches into place using an appliqué stitch and Aurifil Monofilament (1000 mt). If you decide to use raw-edge patches, omit the seam allowance, and sew them into place using a neutral-color thread (we recommend Aurifil color #6711) that will blend in and not interfere with the visual effect of the sashiko stitching.

Note: Appliqué Stitch

The appliqué stitch is a setting many modern machines have; it's a straight line with a zigzag every so often. You sew next to the patch on the base fabric, and the zigzag catches the edge of the patch to hold it down.

SASHIKO

Water has always played a big part in our lives. Living in Seattle, we spend a lot of time meandering along the shores of Puget Sound. Like sashiko artists from centuries ago, we took this symbol that meant so much to us and decided to do a hand-drawn representation of waves on this vest. Feel free to draw something that inspires you. The idea is to use the individual lines of moyouzashi to fully tack down all the patches.

1. Choose your overall sashiko theme or select individual patterns from the Sashiko Stitch Directory *(page 84).*

2. Using a fabric pen or washable pen or pencil, lay out and draw a base grid or trace a template over the section you want to stitch. If you are drawing your own art, now is the time to put washable pen to fabric.

3. Measure and draw in your armhole opening from the cutting diagram *(page 136)*. *Do not cut the armhole openings yet.* As you make your sashiko stitches, do not stitch over the armhole openings or you will be cutting your sashiko threads when you cut the armholes open later.

4. Stitch away. For tips on starting and ending rows see Unshin: Handling the Needle *(page 56)*.

Note: Making the Vest Reversible

We used knotless starts and stops to leave clean stitching lines on both sides of the vest. See To Knot or Not? (page 47).

A look at the finished jacket's right side

A look at the finished jacket's wrong side. Since the edges are finished and we used knotless starts and stops as we stitched, this side looks as good as the right side. When we put the jacket on, we simply fold over the top edge to make the large collar.

ARMHOLES

For the purpose of this tutorial, the orange fabric simulates the body of your vest. The purple is the facing you are creating.

Create the Facing and Cut Armholes

1. If your armhole markings have worn off during stitching, mark them again on the wrong side of the garment.

2. Draw a line matching the armhole depth on the wrong side of an armhole facing rectangle. Make sure this line is centered on the fabric, or your finished facing will come out lopsided. (And that just ain't cute.) *fig. A*

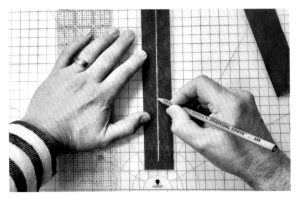

A. For the purpose of this tutorial, the orange fabric in the next set of photos simulates the body of your vest. The purple strip is the armhole facing. We made our armhole facing in the same fabric as the vest.

3. Lay the facing on the garment, wrong sides together, and match up the armhole lines.

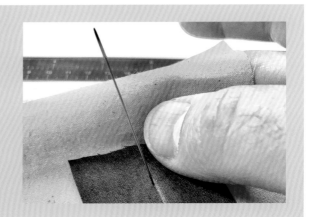

Tip: Use Pins

Draw a dot at the top and bottom of the marked lines of both pieces of fabric. Place a pin through the garment fabric from the right side, perpendicular to the table. Then line up the dot on the facing fabric to the pin, again keeping the wrong sides of fabric facing each other. Push the pin through the facing fabric's dot from behind. Do the same for the bottom dots and voilà, you have lined up your cutting line!

4. Pin the facing into place. *fig. B*

5. Machine stitch using an edge-stitch foot, (10C for BERNINA machines). Move the needle position 2 steps to the left so you will sew close to the left edge of the marked line. This is where the magic comes in: once you have adjusted your needle position, follow your marked line with the foot's guide (that's coming in the next step). If you do not have an edge foot, do your best to stitch as close as possible to 1/16″ (2 mm) from the line. *fig. C*

6. Straight stitch along one side of the marked line. Allow the guide in the center of the foot to move down the middle of the marked line so your stitches are just to the left. You'll have a perfectly stitched edge every time. *Woo-hoo!*

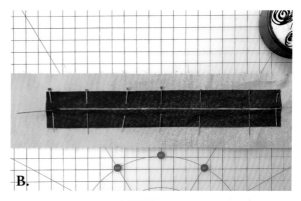

B.

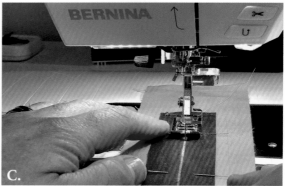

C.

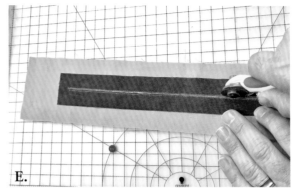

Lift the foot without cutting the thread. Turn the work to sew down the opposite side of the marked line. *fig. D*

7. Using a rotary cutter or scissors, cut the armhole opening through *both the garment and the facing. fig. E*

8. Fold the cut edge of the facing to the sew line approximately ¼″ (6 mm) and press. *fig. F*

9. Turn the entire facing fabric through the opening to the right side of the garment fabric. Give yourself time for this. It'll feel like you are doing something wrong at first, but push on through! Press the long edges of the facing as you turn it to make the turn easier. Pin as needed in preparation for sewing. *figs. G-H*

10. Go back to the sewing machine and snug the outside edge of the facing against the guide of the edge-stitch foot. Sew around the outside edge of the facing with a –2 needle setting. *fig. I*

I.

11. Use a chalk pencil to mark the top and bottom of the opening. This makes it easier to see where you will place the bar-tack stitching. (A *bar tack* is a set of stitches that are sewn across an opening as reinforcement to keep it from tearing due to stress.) Machine or hand sew a bar tack at both ends of the opening. *figs. J-K*

12. Trim the threads and press. *Ta-da!* One fully functioning armhole!

13. Repeat Steps 2–12 for the second armhole.

J.

▌ FINISHING TOUCHES

Vest Edges

1. With the patched side of the vest facing up, make a ½″ (1.2 cm) fold toward the right side of the vest around each edge. Press in place.

2. Fold the edge over another ½″ (1.2 cm) to encase the raw edges. Press and pin into place.

3. Topstitch along the inside edge of the folded seam ⅛″ (3 mm)—*or*—hand stitch around the edge using a ladder stitch *(page 74)* to close the seam.

K.

This vest can be worn right side up or upside down, and if your sashiko stitching is clean and does not have knots, the vest is reversible! If you want to wear your vest closed, use a large shawl pin or kilt pin to close the front.

Rectangle Wrap Vest, worn inside out with boro patches forming a beautiful collar

LOTUS POND THROW

Finished throw: 42″ × 60″ (106.7 × 152.4 cm)

HERE, THE WORLD OF OUR ANCESTORS AND THE WORLD OF TRADITIONAL JAPANESE BORO AND SASHIKO COMBINE in our modern take on quilting using boro and sashiko techniques. This quilt evolved over its creation seemingly on its own. We started with the colors and forms, and as we built the piece, we started seeing the patches as the boards on a small dock built out into a lily pond we frequent here in our local arboretum. Who are we to argue with a project that speaks out so clearly about itself? So we went with it, choosing sashiko patterns that built on the idea of wooden planks, and we created an abstract representation of lotus flowers to complete the lotus pond quilt.

Materials

> ### Note: Fabrics We Used
> *We used a variety of cottons from Michael Miller Fabrics (MM) for the large patches and Michael Miller Cotton Couture (MMCC) yardage for the throw body and scraps for the smaller boro patches. We turned under the edges of the large patches only. You can turn under all, some, or none of the patches as whimsy dictates.*

LIGHT COTTON OR MUSLIN: 2 yards (1.8 m) each for front and back of MMCC in color SC5333-INKX-D

RANDOM FABRIC SCRAPS FOR PATCHES: Enough to cover main areas of your throw plus a few extra smaller patches

PATCH 1: 1 yard (0.9 m) of MM Aquarelle Stripe in neutral

PATCH 2: ⅜ yard (0.3 m) of MMCC in color SC5333-CINN-D

PATCH 3: ⅝ yard (0.6 m) of MM Painters Canvas in terra cotta

PATCH 4: 2 fat quarters (45.7 × 55.9 cm) of MM Bohemian Rhapsody in thyme

PATCH 5: ⅓ yard (0.3 m) of MM Painters Canvas in lime

PATCH 6: ¼ yard (0.2 m) of MMCC in color SC5333-ARMY-D

PATCHES 7 AND 8: Fat eighth or scrap at least 6″ × 6″ (15.2 × 15.2 cm) for each from MM Krystal in blue

VARIOUS SMALLER PATCHES (We used various scraps of Michael Miller Cotton Couture, Bohemian Rhapsody, and Painters Canvas.)

SASHIKO THREAD: Aurifil 12-weight cotton thread in the color(s) of your choice or other sashiko thread *(page 24)*

Cutting

LIGHT COTTON OR MUSLIN: Cut a rectangle 43″ × 61″ (109.2 × 154.9 cm) for both the front and the back.

PATCH 1: Cut a square 32″ × 32″ (81.3 × 81.3 cm).

PATCH 2: Cut a rectangle 11″ × 31″ (27.9 × 78.7 cm).

PATCH 3: Cut a rectangle 17″ × 22″ (43.2 × 55.9 cm).

PATCH 4: Cut a square 12″ × 12″ (30.5 × 30.5 cm).

PATCH 5: Cut a rectangle 10¼″ × 17½″ (26 × 44.5 cm).

PATCH 6: Cut a rectangle 4½″ × 20½″ (11.4 × 52.1 cm).

PATCHES 7 AND 8: For each, cut a square 6″ × 6″ (15.2 × 15.2 cm).

VARIOUS SMALLER PATCHES: Cut later as you see the need.

█ Construction

Seam allowances are ½″ (1.2 cm) unless otherwise noted.

▌ BORO PATCHES

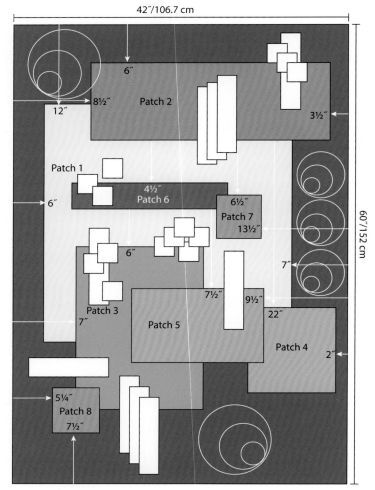

Patch placement

1. Turn the edges of the boro patches under ½″ (1.2 cm) and press.

2. Place the patches on the right side of fabric as shown in the patch placement diagram (*at left*) and pin.

3. Machine baste the boro patches into place. Glue basting will not hold up here. Machine baste— trust us!

THROW ASSEMBLY

1. Right sides facing, pin the front and back panels together.

2. Sew around both long sides, the top, and half of the bottom edge.

3. Clip the corners flat about ⅛″ (3 mm) from the sewn line. This helps the corners come out sharp when the throw is turned.

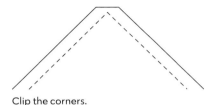

Clip the corners.

4. Turn the throw right side out through the opening on the bottom.

5. Finger-press the seams flat to make sure the sides are straight and the corners are sharp.

Tip: Use That Yardstick

Insert a yardstick into the center of the throw. Push it into the corners and run it along the edges to ensure all seams are fully turned and straight. If you don't have a yardstick, a small-diameter dowel will do.

6. Quickly press to set all the seams.

7. Use the ladder stitch *(page 74)* to close the opening.

8. Lay the throw flat and hand baste the front to the back in preparation for stitching. The idea is to keep the layers of fabric from moving around while you stitch.

SASHIKO STITCHING/QUILTING

All stitching is now done through the patches and the front and back of the throw. For tips on hiding the ends of your lines in the interior of the throw, see To Knot or Not? (page 47).

1. Outline the basted patches 1–8 with running stitches.

2. Lay flat and add any other raw-edge patches as needed. Check out the placement diagram *(previous page)* for our suggested layout.

3. Outline all raw-edge patches.

4. Draw large and small lotus motifs on the front of the throw. We used 3 sizes of circles, aligned at one side, for each lotus shape.

5. Draw any other sashiko motifs you like to fully secure the boro patches.

6. Stitch the lotus and sashiko motifs.

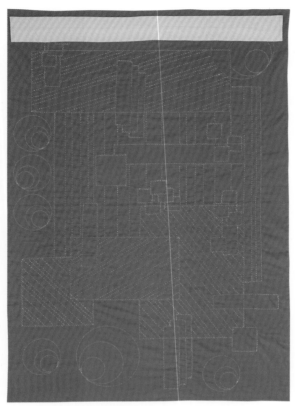

The back of the Lotus Pond Throw. We used diagonal moyouzashi lines ½″ (.2 cm) apart on some of the larger patches and followed the vertical lines provided by the fabric print.

Use and enjoy your new throw ... think about what you want your next one to be!

▌ *OPTIONAL:* MAKE A ROD POCKET

If you wish to display your throw on a wall, you can add a rod pocket for ease of display.

1. Cut a rectangle 9″ × 41″ (22.9 × 104.1 cm) from the same fabric as the back panel. Fold the short edges under ¼″ (6 mm), then another ¼″ (6 mm), and press.

2. Topstitch the folded edge.

3. Fold the rod pocket in half, right sides together widthwise, and sew a ½″ (1.2 cm) seam along the long edge.

4. Turn the rod pocket right side out and press flat with the seam centered on what will be the back of the rod pocket.

5. With the rod pocket oriented horizontally, pull the top layer of fabric down, moving the top fold line ½″ (1.2 cm) toward the center. Press a new fold line. This will create a bubble of fabric that will allow the hanging rod to be inserted without distorting the front of the throw.

6. Measure 1″ (2.5 cm) down from the top of the throw and hand sew both the top and bottom edges of the rod pocket into place.

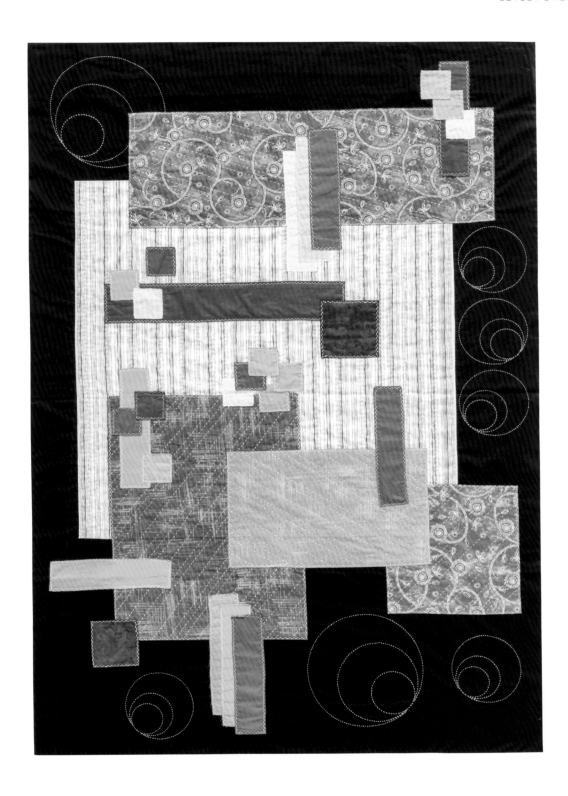

KIMONO-INSPIRED
LONG JACKET

Finished long jacket: Small (M, L, XL, 2X, 3X, 4X, 5X)
See the cutting chart *(page 152)* for size measurements.

THE DESIGN FOR THIS JACKET WAS INSPIRED BY THE KIMONO, FISHER, AND FIREFIGHTER COATS WE STUDIED. Unlike the other pieces in this book, we did not include any boro patchwork but instead showcased the way sashiko builds up a simple fabric. The fabric we chose is a densely woven thread-dyed black fabric from Michael Miller Fabrics. We loved how the dense weave and the deep black color let the stitching pop to show off the lines of sashiko. The sashiko stitching is a combination of traditional patterns and our own modern interpretation of the quilting sashiko we saw on long jackets with layers of fabric.

Materials

BLACK SOLID: 4 (4, 4½, 5, 5, 5½, 5½, 5½) yards / 3.7 (3.7, 4.1, 4.6, 4.6, 5, 5, 5) m
(We used Michael Miller Fabrics Cotton Couture in jet black.)

SASHIKO THREAD: Aurifil 12-weight cotton thread in the color(s) of your choice or other sashiko thread *(page 24)* (We used red for outlining the patches and our variegated orange, color 4657, for the allover stitching.)

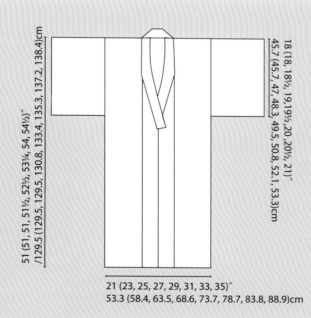

51 (51, 51, 51½, 52½, 53¼, 54, 54½)" / 129.5 (129.5, 129.5, 130.8, 133.4, 135.3, 137.2, 138.4)cm

18 (18, 18½, 19,19½, 20, 20½, 21)" 45.7 (45.7, 47, 48.3, 49.5, 50.8, 52.1, 53.3)cm

21 (23, 25, 27, 29, 31, 33, 35)"
53.3 (58.4, 63.5, 68.6, 73.7, 78.7, 83.8, 88.9)cm

PATTERN NOTES

- To keep the seams from fraying as you stitch the individual pieces, we recommend serging the body pieces using a 3-needle overlock or zigzag stitch along the edge.

- This jacket is not lined. Pressing finished seams will give you a polished look and keep the edges clean.

- The right side and wrong side in this pattern refer to which side is worn to the public.

Cutting

KIMONO COMPONENTS: Cut the components according to the sizes in the cutting chart *(below)*. See the front panel diagram *(below)* for cutting the diagonal edge.

	S	M	L	XL
Bust measurement *(Use to find your size.)*	32" (81.3 cm)	36" (91.4 cm)	40" (101.6 cm)	44" (111.8 cm)
Back panel width × height	22" × 52¾" (55.9 × 134 cm)	24" × 52¾" (61 × 134 cm)	26" × 53¾ (66 × 136.5 cm)	28" × 53¼" (71.1 × 135.3 cm)
Main front panels *(Cut 2.)*	8¼" × 52¾" (21 × 134 cm)	9" × 52¾" (22.9 × 134 cm)	9¾" × 53¾" (24.8 × 136.5 cm)	10¾" × 53¼" (27.3 × 135.3 cm)
Inner front panels* *(Cut 2. See diagram, below.)*	4¼" × 20½" / 42" (10.8 × 52.1 / 106.7 cm)	4½" × 20½" / 42" (11.4 × 52 / 106.7 cm)	4¾" × 20½" / 42" (12.1 × 52.1 / 106.7 cm)	4¾" × 20½" / 42¼" (12.1 × 52.1 / 107.3 cm)
Collar	5" × 51½" (12.7 × 130.8 cm)	5" × 52" (12.7 × 132.1 cm)	5" × 52½" (12.7 × 133.4 cm)	5" × 53" (12.7 × 134.6 cm)
Sleeves** *(Cut 2.)*	36" × 14" (91.4 × 35.5 cm)	36" × 14½" (91.4 × 36.8 cm)	37" × 15½" (94 × 39.4 cm)	38" × 16" (96.5 × 40.6 cm)
Armhole depth***	9" (22.9 cm)	9" (22.9 cm)	9½" (24.1 cm)	10" (25.4 cm)

4¼ (4½, 4¾, 4¾, 4¼, 5¼, 5¼, 5¾)" /10.8 (11.4, 12, 12, 13, 13.3, 13.3, 14.6) cm

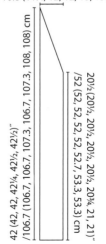

42 (42, 42, 42¼, 42½, 42½)" /106.7 (106.7, 106.7, 107.3, 108, 108) cm

20½ (20½, 20½, 20½, 20½, 20¾, 21, 21)" /52 (52, 52, 52, 52, 52.7, 53.3, 53.3) cm

Cutting the inside front panel

* The 3 measurements are width × inside length / outside length. See the cutting diagram to cut one end of each inner front panel at an angle between the inside and outside lengths. If your fabric has a right and wrong side, take care to cut 1 panel with the angle pointing to the left and the second with the angle pointing to the right.

** Sleeves include a 2½" (6.4 cm) seam allowance on the cuff fold.

*** Wait until you have sewn the shoulder seams together; then mark the armhole depth from the seamline (see Sleeves, page 155).

	2X	3X	4X	5X
Bust measurement *(Use to find your size.)*	48″ (121.9 cm)	52″ (132.1 cm)	56″ (142.2 cm)	60″ (152.4 cm)
Back panel width × height	30″ × 54¼″ (76.2 × 137.8 cm)	32″ × 55″ (81.3 × 139.7 cm)	34″ × 55¾″ (86.4 × 141.6 cm)	36″ × 56¼″ (91.4 × 142.9 cm)
Main front panels *(Cut 2.)*	11¼″ × 54¼″ (28.6 × 137.8 cm)	12¼″ × 55″ (31.1 × 139.7 cm)	13¼″ × 55¾″ (33.6 × 141.6 cm)	13¾″ × 56¼″ (34.9 × 142.9 cm)
Inner front panels* *(Cut 2. See diagram, previous page.)*	5″ × 20½″ / 42″ (12.7 × 52.1 / 106.7 cm)	5¼″ × 20¾″ / 42¼″ (13.3 × 52.7 / 107.3 cm)	5¼″ × 21″ / 42½″ (13.3 × 53.3 / 108 cm)	5¾″ × 21″ / 42½″ (14.6 × 53.3 / 108 cm)
Collar	5″ × 53½″ (12.7 × 136 cm)	5″ × 53¾″ (12.7 × 136.6 cm)	5″ × 53¾″ (12.7 × 136.6 cm)	5″ × 55″ (12.7 × 139.7 cm)
Sleeves** *(Cut 2.)*	39″ × 16½″ (99.1 × 41.9 cm)	40″ × 17″ (101.6 × 43.2 cm)	41″ × 17¾″ (104.1 × 45.1 cm)	42″ × 17¾″ (106.7 × 45.1 cm)
Armhole depth***	10½″ (26.7 cm)	11″ (27.9 cm)	11½″ (29.2 cm)	12″ (30.5 cm)

▮ Construction

Seam allowances are ½″ (1.2 cm) unless otherwise noted.

▮ SASHIKO STITCHING

1. Mark out a grid on each area or draw templates. Leave a small unstitched space, ¼″ to ½″ (0.6 to 1.2 cm), around the edge of each piece. This is how we marked and stitched our jacket:

• **Back panel:** Moyouzashi running stitch, in rows ½″ (1.2 cm) apart (see the diagram, *at right*). Inside the open square, we stitched Linked Seven Treasures *(page 97)* stitched on a 1″ (2.5 cm) grid.

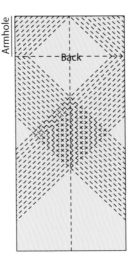

Back panels stitched in moyouzashi running stitch ½″ (.2 cm) apart *(page 85)*. 45° in one direction from center back neck to the base of the armhole then alternate to negative 45°. Mirror image stitching on the left side.

- **Sleeves:** Woven stitch 1 *(page 94)* in a 6″ (15.2 cm) strip across the cuff end of the sleeve (see the diagram, *at right*). Leave a ½″ (1.2 cm) seam allowance on the shoulder and body connection seam. The cuff fold includes a 2½″ (6.4 cm) seam allowance.

- **Front panels:** Persimmon flower *(page 90)*

- **Collar:** Woven stitch 1 *(page 94)*

Tip: Pattern Stitches on Collar

When marking and stitching the sashiko patterns to the collar, begin at the center and work outward to the left end of the collar, then again from the center to the right end. This will ensure your pattern will be centered on the collar.

2. Stitch the sashiko patterns onto the jacket components.

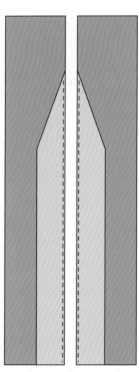

6″/15.2 cm

Sleeve

6″ (5.2 cm) of sleeves are stitched in woven stitch 1 *(page 94)*. Folded to 3″ (7.6 cm) when assembled.

█ JACKET BODY ASSEMBLY

1. Right sides together, pin and sew the right inner front panel to the right main front panel along the long edge. Align the straight short edge of the inner panel with the bottom of the main front panel.

2. Repeat for the left panel.

3. Right sides together, sew the shoulder seams, attaching the front panels to the back panel.

4. Press the shoulder seams open.

Sew the main front panels to the inner front panels.

▌ SLEEVES

Attach the Sleeves

1. On the right side of the garment body, measure and mark the armhole depth listed in the cutting directions *(page 152)*. Measure from the shoulder seam and mark both the back and front panels.

2. Lay the garment body open, right side up.

3. Set in the sleeves as follows:

- Fold the sleeve in half lengthwise and mark the center.

- Right sides together, match the center mark on the sleeve to the shoulder seam and pin into place.

- Pin the sleeve to the body at the measured armhole depth marks on the front and back panels.

- Continue to pin as needed along the seam.

4. Sew the sleeve to the body of the jacket between the armhole depth marks.

5. Repeat Steps 1–4 with the second sleeve.

Make the Sleeve Cuffs

1. With the wrong side facing up, fold and press a ½″ (1.2 cm) seam allowance along the end of the sleeve.

2. Make another fold, this time 2″ (5.1 cm), and press to make a 2″ (5.1 cm) cuff.

3. Using a blind hem stitch, sew along the edge of the fold to secure the seam.

4. Repeat Steps 1–3 for the opposite sleeve.

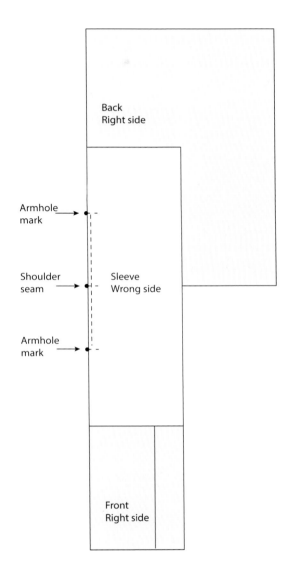

Sew the Sides and Sleeve Flags

Sleeve flags   *The flags are the parts of the sleeve that lie next to the body of the garment but do not attach. Instead, they hang down, like a flag.*

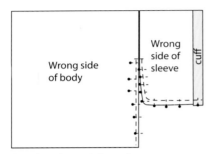

Sew the sides and sleeve flags.

1. Turn the kimono inside out so the right sides of the sleeve and the body of the kimono are facing each other.

2. Pin the side seams of the kimono body together up to the sleeve opening, making sure not to pin the sleeve flags to the body.

3. Pin along the underside seam of the sleeves and up along the sleeve flag to the armhole opening. Again, the sleeve flags do not connect to the body panel.

4. Starting from the cuff, sew the underside seam along the sleeve flag, being sure not to sew it to the body of the kimono. Turn the corner at the end of the sleeve flag and sew up to the armhole opening.

5. Starting from the bottom of the garment, sew the side seam to the armhole opening. Remember to backstitch at the beginning and ending of your lines of sewing.

6. Repeat Steps 2–5 for the opposite side.

▌BOTTOM HEM

1. With the wrong side facing, fold and press a ¼″ (6 mm) seam along the bottom hem.

2. Fold and press another 1″ (2.5 cm) seam to encase the raw edge.

3. Pin into place and sew.

▌COLLAR

1. With the wrong side facing up, press a ½″ (1.2 cm) seam allowance along one long edge and the 2 short edges of the collar. If you added sashiko stitching to the collar, press the seam allowance on the long edge that is not close to the stitching.

2. Press a lengthwise fold in the collar.

3. Fold the collar in half lengthwise and mark the center with a pin or marking pen.

4. Mark the center back of the neckline.

5. Right sides together, pin the center mark on the collar to the center mark on the neckline. Be sure you are pinning the side of the collar without the pressed seam allowance.

6. Working from the center out, pin the rest of the collar in place.

7. Sew the first side of the collar into place.

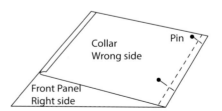

Tip: Easy Does It!

When sewing the collar into place, sew just like you pinned—from the center out—to ensure the collar lies evenly along the neckline.

8. Press the seam to the collar side.

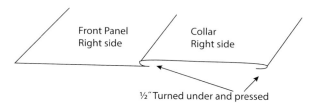

Front Panel Right side

Collar Right side

½" Turned under and pressed

9. Fold the collar in half lengthwise along the pressed line so half of the right side is facing out.

10. Pin into place as before.

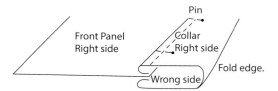

Pin

Front Panel Right side

Collar Right side

Wrong side

Fold edge.

11. Hand stitch using a ladder stitch *(page 74)* or machine topstitch the collar into place, encasing the first seam.

12. Sew the bottom edge of the collar closed using a blind hem or slip stitch.

▌FINAL TOUCHES

Wash and press to remove the sashiko stitching lines.

Wear your long jacket with pride!

HANTEN SHORT JACKET

Finished jacket: Small (M, L, XL, 2X, 3X, 4X, 5X)
See cutting chart *(page 160)* for fitting measurements.

FOR THIS BOOK WE WANTED TO INCLUDE A JACKET THAT HAD A PRACTICAL, EVERYDAY USE. The compact style of the traditional hanten jacket makes it easy to throw on and coordinate with everything from casual to dressier outfits, depending on the textiles you use. We chose a modern take on boro patchwork, using patches of the same fabric as the main body of the jacket and thread that coordinates with the color of the glorious red Brussels Washer Linen fabric.

The moment we touched it, we knew we had to have it. However, the glorious red fabric we used for our short jacket design—a 55/45 linen/rayon blend—is "slick" in relation to the sashiko stitches. Sashiko running stitches worked through one layer of this fabric were a challenge because of the natural give in the weave of the fabric. No way no how we were giving up on this fabric ... we were smitten! We decided to either use a lining fabric like muslin or simply use two layers of the same fabric but turn the fabric 90° when cutting the second piece, giving us a layering piece cut across the grain. We then glue basted the two layers together and zig-zagged the edges, resulting in a two-layered fabric that was sashiko-stitched as a single piece. That second layer worked beautifully. Issue fixed and the continuity of this gorgeous, must-have fabric was maintained. *Ta-da!*

Materials

LINEN: 2¼ (2¼, 2¼, 2½, 2½, 2¾, 2¾, 2¾) yards /
2.1 (2.1, 2.1, 2.3, 2.3, 2.5, 2.5, 2.5) m
This includes both layers of the jacket and the boro patches (We used Robert Kaufman's Brussels Washer Linen in Poppy.)

GLUE STICK

SASHIKO THREAD: Aurifil 12-weight cotton thread in the color(s) of your choice or other sashiko thread *(page 24)*
(We used a variegated thread for the geometric stitch pattern and thread that matched the fabric to outline the boro patches.)

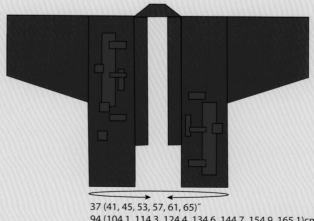

37 (41, 45, 53, 57, 61, 65)"
94 (104.1, 114.3, 124.4, 134.6, 144.7, 154.9, 165.1)cm
Finished sizes

- -

PATTERN NOTES

- This jacket is not lined. It has 2 layers of fabric, but since we stitched the sashiko through both layers before we assembled the jacket, there will be inside seams. To keep the seams from fraying, we recommend serging the body pieces using a 3-needle overlock or zigzag stitch along the edge.

- Right side and wrong side in this pattern refer to which side is worn to the public.

- -

Cutting

JACKET COMPONENTS: Cut the components according to the sizes in the cutting chart *(below)*. If you want to double the fabric, as we did, cut 2 of each component—front, back, collar, left sleeve, and right sleeve, with one piece cut on grain and the second cut on the bias.

	S	M	L	XL
Bust measurement *(Use to find your size.)*	32" (81.3 cm)	36" (91.4 cm)	40" (101.6 cm)	44" (111.8 cm)
Finished bust	34" (86.4 cm)	38" (96.5 cm)	42" (106.7 cm)	46" (116.8 cm)
Back panel	19½" × 27" (49.5 × 68.6 cm)	21½" × 27½" (54.6 × 69.9 cm)	23½" × 28" (59.7 × 71.1 cm)	25½" × 28½" (64.8 × 72.4 cm)
Front panels	7" × 27" (17.8 × 68.6 cm)	7¾" × 27½" (19.7 × 69.9 cm)	8½" × 28" (21.6 × 71.1 cm)	9½" × 28½" (24.1 × 72.4 cm)
Collar	5" × 47" (12.7 × 119.4 cm)	5" × 48" (12.7 × 121.9 cm)	5" × 49" (12.7 × 124.5 cm)	5" × 50" (12.7 × 127 cm)
Sleeves*	14½" × 10" / 14" (36.8 × 25.4 / 35.6 cm)	14¾" × 10" / 14" (37.5 × 25.4 / 35.6 cm)	15" × 10½" / 14" (38.1 × 26.7 / 35.6 cm)	15¼" × 11" / 14" (38.7 × 27.9 / 35.6 cm)
Armhole depth**	14" (35.6 cm)	14" (35.6 cm)	14" (35.6 cm)	14" (35.6 cm)

* The 3 measurements are width × width at cuff / width at body. See the cutting diagram (next page) to cut the bottom at an angle between the cuff and body, leaving a ½" (1.2 cm) at the top of the sleeve.

** Wait to mark the armhole depth until you have stitched the front and back panels together (see Add the Sleeves, page 164).

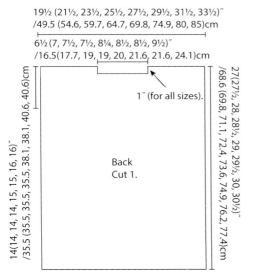

Cutting the back

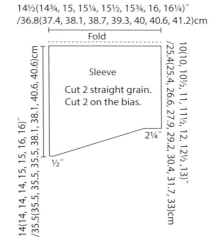

Cutting the sleeves

	2X	3X	4X	5X
Bust measurement *(Use to find your size.)*	48″ (121.9 cm)	52″ (132.1 cm)	56″ (142.2 cm)	60″ (152.4 cm)
Finished bust	50″ (127 cm)	54″ (137.2 cm)	58″ (147.3 cm)	62″ (157.5 cm)
Back panel	27½″ × 29″ (69.9 × 73.6 cm)	29½″ × 29½″ (74.9 × 74.9 cm)	31½″ × 30″ (80 × 76.2 cm)	33½″ × 30½″ (85 × 77.4 cm)
Front panels	10¼″ × 29″ (26 × 73.7 cm)	11″ × 29½″ (27.9 × 74.9 cm)	12″ × 30″ (30.5 × 76.2 cm)	12½″ × 30½″ (31.8 × 77.5 cm)
Collar	5″ × 52″ (12.7 × 132.1 cm)	5″ × 53″ (12.7 × 134.6 cm)	5″ × 53″ (12.7 × 134.6 cm)	5″ × 55″ (12.7 × 139.7 cm)
Sleeves*	15½″ × 11½″ / 15″ (39.4 × 29.2 / 38.1 cm)	15¾″ × 12″ / 15″ (40 × 30.5 / 38.1 cm)	16″ × 12½″ / 16″ (40.6 × 31.8 / 40.6 cm)	16¼″ × 13″ / 16″ (41.3 × 33 / 40.6 cm)
Armhole depth**	15″ (38.1 cm)	15″ (38.1 cm)	16″ (40.6 cm)	16″ (40.6 cm)

Patches

We used these sizes of patches. Adjust and make as many or few patches as you like.

BACK PATCHES:

- Cut 2 rectangles 3″ × 6½″ (7.6 × 16.5 cm).

- Cut 1 rectangle 2″ × 6½″ (5.1 × 16.5 cm).

- Cut 2 squares 3½″ × 3½″ (8.9 × 8.9 cm).

- Cut 3 squares 3″ × 3″ (7.6 × 7.6 cm).

- Cut 2 rectangles 2″ × 4″ (5.1 × 10.2 cm).

- Cut 2 squares 2½″ × 2½″ (6.4 × 6.4 cm).

- Cut 2 squares 2″ × 2″ (5.1 × 5.1 cm).

- Cut 2 rectangles 1½″ × 4½″ (3.8 × 11.4 cm).

- Cut 1 rectangle 1½″ × 4″ (3.8 × 10.2 cm).

- Cut 1 rectangle 2″ × 4″ (5.1 × 10.2 cm).

FRONT PATCHES:

- Cut 3 rectangles 1½″ × 3½″ (3.8 × 8.9 cm).

- Cut 6 squares 2″ × 2″ (5.1 × 5.1 cm).

- Cut 4 rectangles 1″ × 4″ (2.5 × 10.2 cm).

- Cut 1 rectangle 2″ × 4″ (5.1 × 10.2 cm).

Back of Hanten Short Jacket

Construction

BORO AND SASHIKO

1. Arrange the patches on the front and back panel. Play with the layout until you like what you see. The boro placement diagrams *(below)* show the placement of the patches for our sample, using the sizes listed in the cutting directions *(previous page)*.

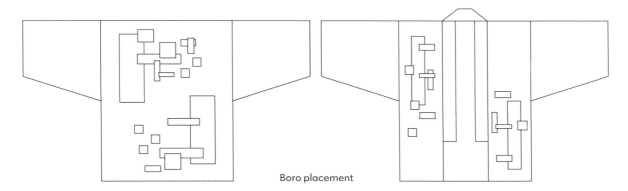

Boro placement

2. Baste the patches to the front and back panels.

3. Mark out a sashiko grid on each area or trace from templates. The sashiko placement diagrams *(below)* show how we stitched our jacket.

4. Stitch sashiko patterns onto the jacket.

Collar / Star Stitch *(page 93)*

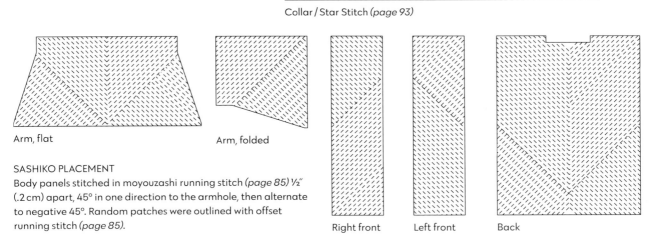

Arm, flat

Arm, folded

SASHIKO PLACEMENT
Body panels stitched in moyouzashi running stitch *(page 85)* ½˝ (.2 cm) apart, 45° in one direction to the armhole, then alternate to negative 45°. Random patches were outlined with offset running stitch *(page 85)*.

Right front   Left front   Back

Tip: Pattern Stitches on the Collar

When stitching sashiko patterns to the collar, begin stitching at the center and work outward to the left end of the collar; then again from the center to the right end. This will ensure your pattern will be centered on the collar.

▌JACKET BODY ASSEMBLY

1. With right sides together, sew the shoulder seams. Start from the outside shoulder and work to the inside, attaching the front panels to the back panel. There will be ½″ (1.2 cm) on the inside front panel that is not sewn.

2. Press the shoulder seams open.

3. On the front inside edge of both the right front and left front panels, fold over ½″ (1.2 cm) to the wrong side; press.

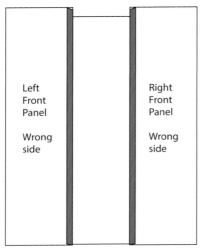

Press the front panel inside edge seam.

Add the Sleeves

1. On the right side of the garment body, measure and mark the armhole depth listed in the cutting directions *(page 160)*. Measure from the shoulder seam, and mark both the front and back panels.

2. Lay the garment body open, right side up.

3. Set in the sleeves as follows:

- Fold the sleeve in half lengthwise and mark the center.

- Right sides together, match the center mark on the sleeve to the shoulder seam and pin in place.

- Pin the end of the sleeve to the armhole depth marks on the front and back panels.

- Continue to pin as needed along the seam.

4. Sew the sleeve to the body of the jacket.

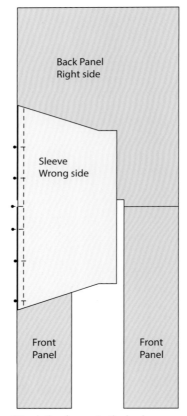

Attach the sleeves to the body.

5. Turn the jacket inside out so the right side of the sleeve and the body of the jacket are facing. Pin the side seams and the underside seam of the sleeve.

6. Starting from the bottom of the garment, sew the side seam up to the sleeve opening, then pivot and continue to sew along the bottom seam of the sleeve.

7. Repeat Steps 1–6 for the second sleeve.

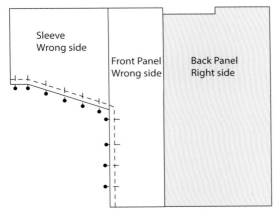

Sew the sides and underside of the sleeves.

▌ MAKE THE SLEEVE CUFFS

1. With the wrong side facing, press the undersleeve seam open.

2. Press a ¼″ (6 mm) seam allowance along the cuff.

3. Fold and press another 1″ (2.5 cm) seam allowance along the cuff.

4. Sew the folded hem using a blind hem stitch to secure the seam.

5. Repeat Steps 1–4 for the opposite sleeve.

▌ BOTTOM HEM

1. With the wrong sides facing, fold and press a ¼″ (6 mm) seam along the bottom hem.

2. Fold and press another 1″ (2.5 cm) seam, covering the previous ¼″ (6 mm).

3. Pin into place and sew.

▌ ATTACH THE COLLAR

1. With the wrong side facing up, press a ½″ (1.2 cm) seam allowance along one long edge and the 2 short edges of the collar.

2. Press a lengthwise fold in the collar.

3. Fold the collar in half crosswise and mark the center with a pin or marking pen.

4. Mark the center back of the neckline.

5. Right sides together, pin the center mark on the collar to the center mark on the neckline. Be sure you are pinning the side of the collar without the pressed seam allowance.

6. Working from the center out, pin the rest of the collar in place.

7. Sew the first side of the collar in place.

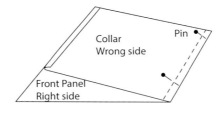

Tip: Easy Does It!

When sewing the collar into place, sew just like you pinned—from the center out—to ensure the collar lies evenly along the neckline.

8. Press the seam to the collar side.

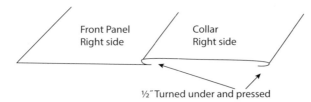

Front Panel
Right side

Collar
Right side

½" Turned under and pressed

9. Fold the collar in half lengthwise along the pressed line so the right side is facing out.

10. Pin into place as before.

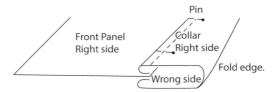

Pin

Front Panel
Right side

Collar
Right side

Fold edge.

Wrong side

11. Hand stitch using a ladder stitch *(page 74)* or machine topstitch the collar into place, encasing the first seam. Continue sewing a ¼" (6 mm) seam down the front inside edge of the front panel that was previously pressed.

12. Sew the bottom edge of the collar closed using a blind hem or slip stitch.

▋ FINAL TOUCHES

Launder as needed to remove any pen/pencil marks.

Wear with pride ... a lot of it!

Detail of the Hanten Short Jacket, showing the allover sashiko stitching in our variegated perle cotton

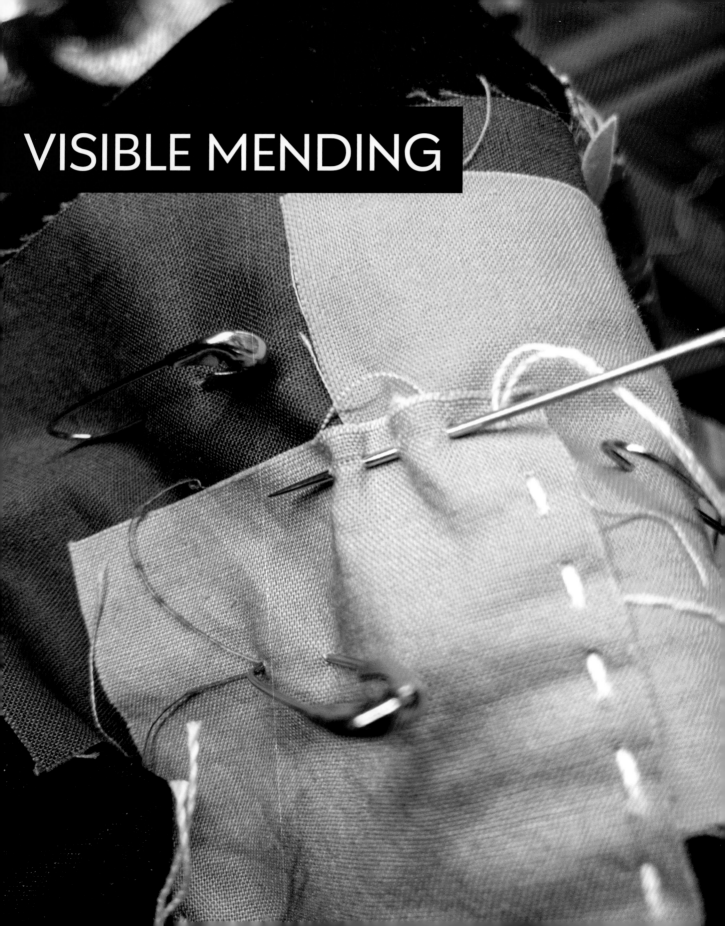

VISIBLE MENDING

The resurgence of the slow-fashion movement has brought about a greater awareness of just how much of a throw-away attitude we have taken regarding our clothes. Something gets a hole or a snag in it, and we throw it out and buy something new. Considering the context of boro and sashiko, they are the perfect remedy to that throw-away habit. Visible mending is simply the practice of using mending and reinforcing techniques on your clothes in such a way that the results are, well, visible. That is exactly what boro and sashiko are!

Materials

FABRIC FOR PATCH: You can be as creative or as understated as you like with this. Any fabric that can be stitched down to cover the area to be mended is fair game. Don't be afraid to play with fabric and thread colors to really put the *visible* in visible mending!

SASHIKO THREAD

SASHIKO NEEDLE

PINS: Straight pins or coiless safety pins. We prefer coiless safety pins because we don't have to apply as many Band-Aids. Just sayin' ...

WASHABLE GLUE: This is our favorite basting method when the fabrics being worked with will not be damaged by the glue. The patch can be placed and moved with ease (no moving around of pins), and the glue washes out, leaving no residue. Please test a small piece of fabric if you are concerned about damaging the fabric you are working with. This can come in sticks, powders, and sprays; we prefer glue sticks *(page 27)*.

▌ THE FIRST BIG DECISION

After you have chosen your patching fabric, think about the stitches you will use to secure the area. While you can use any of the sashiko stitches in this book, you have to consider the final use of the piece you are patching. If the area is worn through from use, you want a fairly strong stitch to reinforce the area as well as the patching. If the hole is a tear, burn, or insect hole, you can use a more decorative stitch without the concern of reinforcement. If the edges of the fabric are likely to fray, use a smaller stitch to prevent the threads of the fabric to be patched from fraying any more.

Random running stitches are our go-to for reinforcement patches. These are small stabs that are close together that really create a "pad" of fabric and stitches.

The extent of the damage will determine whether you need to patch, stitch, or both.

▌ PATCHING WITH STITCHING ALONE

If only a few of the cross threads are broken but the base fabric is still mostly intact, we need to reinforce a weak spot that is not yet threadbare. In this case, you might be able to get away with a grouping of dense stitches like parallel lines of moyouzashi-style running stitches. If this still doesn't seem secure enough, you can also work dense lines of moyouzashi-style running stitch at 90° to the first set of stitches. You can even run some diagonal lines of stitches though the weakened area to further reinforce the base fabric. In these cases, we tend to not pay close attention to the moyouzashi rule of the stitches not crossing on top of the fabric. The goal here is to reinforce the fabric to prevent more threads from breaking.

Parallel lines of running stitches to reinforce a weak area of fabric

A dense network of running stitches locks down the threads of a weak area, preventing further thread breakage and weakening of the area.

▌ PATCHING WITH ADDED FABRIC ALONE

If enough of the cross threads are broken so you can see through all or portions of the area, the weakened area is threadbare and a dense network of stitches may not be sufficient. Likewise, if a threadbare area has broken completely through or an actual hole has been torn in the fabric, it's time to bring a patch into play.

A patch will conceal the hole and prevent further tearing. Your only decision at this point is whether you want the patch on top of the hole or under the hole. The patch on the outside or the inside is an aesthetic preference and easy enough to test by using a little glue stick or pins to hold the patch in place and stand back and see which placement makes you the happiest. After you have made that decision, it's simply a matter of securing the patch.

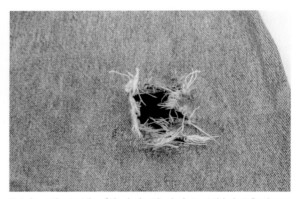

Patch on the inside of the hole. The hole is visible but further tearing is not likely.

A.

B.

C.

Sashiko stitching over the area of the patch

D.

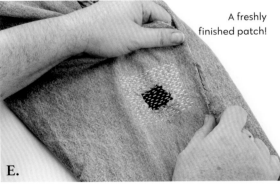

A freshly finished patch!

E.

1. Clean up any unwanted loose threads. Most of the time when we are placing a patch on the inside of a hole or weak spot, we trim off only the really long threads because we like the frayed edges. *fig. A*

2. Place the patch over the hole and glue or pin into place. It helps to turn the garment inside out. *fig. B*

3. If the patch is on the inside of the hole, you will need to place pins or thread baste around the outside edge of the patch so you know where the edges are once you start stitching over them. We prefer thread basting here because pins can interfere with the patching stitches. *fig. C*

4. Turn the garment right side out and stitch over the patch area, working beyond the edges of the patch to secure it properly. Remember, the more dense the stitches, the more secure the area will be. *fig. D*

5. When you are satisfied that the patch is secure, remove the pins or the thread used for basting and enjoy your renewed garment! *fig. E*

If you place your patch on the outside of the hole, you can skip Step 3 and stitch over the patch area as in Step 4.

BIBLIOGRAPHY

▌ COLLECTIONS

Asian art collection, Seattle Art Museum, Seattle, Washington.

Boro collection, Amuse Museum (amusemuseum.com), Asakusa, Tokyo.

Personal collection of Rowland Crawford, Seattle, Washington.

Ginza, Aki. *How to Make*. Translated by Aki Ginza. Self-published, 998.
Note: A collection of Aki Ginza notes and sketches on sashiko and sashiko design.

Sato, Yoshiko. *Tsugaru Kogin Sashiko Design Collection: Hiroko Takahashi, a Gift from the Heavens*. Karashi, 209.

▌ VIDEOS

"The Tokugawa Shogunate: Social and Foreign Policies." Seattle Public Library Streaming Archives, 204. (Go to spl.org > *search* Tokugawa Shogunate > *click on book title under* Books & Media.)

"Japan Under the Shoguns." Seattle Public Library Streaming Archives, 204. (Go to spl.org > *search* Japan Under the Shoguns > *click on book title under* Books & Media.)

▌ BOOKS AND ADDITIONAL READING

Avakian, Monique. *The Meiji Restoration and the Rise of Modern Japan (Turning Points in World History)*. Englewood Cliffs, New Jersey: Silver Burdett Press, 99.

Earl, David Magarey. *Emperor and Nation in Japan: Political Thinkers of the Tokugawa Period*. Seattle: University of Washington Press, 964.
Note: In its original form, submitted as a doctoral dissertation to the faculty of Political Science of Columbia University.

Gordon, Andrew. *A Modern History of Japan: From Tokugawa Times to Present*. 3rd ed. New York: Oxford University Press, 204.

Horikiri, Tatsuichi. *The Stories Clothes Tell: Voices of Working-Class Japan*. Edited and translated by Rieko Wagoner. Lanham, Maryland: Rowman & Littlefield, 206.
Note: Originally published in 990 as a monograph, *Nuno no Inochi (The Life of Clothes)*. Expanded edition. Tokyo: Shinnippon Shuppan-sha, 2004. The present volume is a translation of the 2004 edition.

Mason, Penelope. *History of Japanese Art*. Englewood Cliffs, New Jersey: Prentice-Hall; and New York: Harry N. Abrams, Inc., 993.

Meyer, Milton W. *Japan: A Concise History, Fourth Edition, Updated*. Lanham, Maryland: Rowman & Littlefield, 203.

Swann, Peter C., *A Concise History of Japanese Art*. Tokyo: Kodansha International; New York: distributor, Kodansha International through Harper & Row, 979.
Note: Originally published in 958 under the title *An Introduction to the Arts of Japan*.

Takeda, Sharon Sadako, and Luke Shepherd Roberts. *Japanese Fishermen's Coats from Awaji Island*. Los Angeles: Fowler Museum of Cultural History at UCLA, 200.

United States Centennial Commission. "International Exhibition, 876: Official Catalogue." Philadelphia, Pennsylvania: Published for the Centennial Catalogue Co. by John R. Nagle and Co., 876.

Victoria and Albert Museum. *Embroidery: A Maker's Guide*. New York: Thames & Hudson Inc., 207.

(Multiple contributors). *8th Century Japan: Culture and Society*. Richmond, United Kingdom: Curzon, 2000. Originally published: St. Leonards, New South Wales: Allen & Unwin, 989.
Note: Alternative title: *Eighteenth Century Japan*.

INDEX

ABOUT THE AUTHORS

SHANNON LEIGH ROUDHÁN AND
JASON BOWLSBY are the dynamic DIY duo
from Seattle, Washington.

Shannon and Jason's work is fueled by their
unfettered sense of curiosity, which has led them
to explore a wide cross section of the fiber arts
and other creative arts. The result is a multidisci-
plinary background that allows them to create a
distinctive unified aesthetic that carries across all
their areas of study, design, and classes.

The duo's award-winning crochet, knit, quilting,
handwork, and sewing designs have been featured
in and on the covers of dozens of domestic and
international publications. Together, Shannon
and Jason have published more than 300 patterns
and books.

Their fashion and portrait photography work
can be seen in their patterns and in four of
their books. The duo are sought-after freelance
book-packaging designers, having created books
for major publishing companies like Sterling
Publishing, Leisure Arts, and Creative Publishing.

For over 30 years, Shannon and Jason's enthusiasm,
quirky senses of humor, and relatable teaching
style have made them sought-after teachers in
guilds and in local and national venues, such
as Sew Expo, Houston Quilt Festival, Pacific
International Quilt Festival, and the Bainbridge
Artisan Resource Network (BARN). They also
have a wide range of online classes at Craftsy and
Creative Spark.

Jason and Shannon

Shannon and Jason are proud ambassadors for Aurifil,
BERNINA, Clover, Reliable Corporation, Cherrywood
Hand Dyed Fabrics, and The Daylight Company.

Shannon and Jason have been married for 26 years and
live in Seattle, Washington, with their three Shiba Inu
who, more or less, support their ventures ... as long as
enough time is taken for walks, treats, and the occasional
couch nap.

Visit Jason and Shannon online and follow on social media!
Website: shannonandjason.com
Instagram: @embracethecreativechaos
Twitter: @ShannonandJason
Facebook: /embracethecreativechaos
Pinterest: /embracethecreativechaos

The Shibakidz